AF483262

THE RETIREMENT PERISCOPE

How a Clear Financial Perspective Leads to Better
Preparation and Disciplined Decision-Making

ROB BURNETTE

THE RETIREMENT PERISCOPE
How a Clear Financial Perspective Leads to Better Preparation and Disciplined Decision-Making

ISBN: 979-8-90343-001-7 (Paperback)
         979-8-90343-027-7 (Hardback)
         979-8-90343-002-4 (Kindle eBook)

Expert
Press
www.ExpertPress.net

Editing by Ty Hager
Copyediting by Hannah Skaggs
Proofreading by Abby Kendall
Text design and composition by Emily Fritz
Cover design by Casey Fritz

*For those who feel they cannot afford a financial planner and others
who fear running out of money in retirement . . .
hope is not lost, and clarity is just around the corner for those willing
to act today. My wish for you is fair winds and following seas.*

CONTENTS

UP PERISCOPE!

If you're like most people, retirement planning doesn't scare you because you've done nothing—it unsettles you because you've done *something*, and you're not sure whether it all adds up to enough.

You've worked. You've saved when you could. You've made reasonable decisions with the information you had at the time. And yet, as retirement moves from an abstract idea to something more real, a quiet uncertainty starts to creep in. *Am I actually prepared? Do these pieces work together? What happens if something changes?*

That uncertainty is common. And it's understandable.

The retirement planning landscape is confusing, not because people aren't capable but because the information is fragmented. Investments are discussed in one place, insurance in another, taxes somewhere else entirely. Retirement income often gets pushed down the road as a "later" problem. Most people are never shown how these pieces interact or why decisions in one area can quietly affect outcomes in another.

This book is meant to bring those pieces into focus.

Perspective from Below the Surface

My name is Rob Burnette, and I've spent much of my career thinking in terms of systems, preparation, and risk. Before I ever worked in finance, I served for over two decades in the Navy's submarine community, eventually becoming a chief engineer. On a submarine, clarity matters. You don't get to panic when conditions get rough. You rely on preparation, perspective, and disciplined decision-making.

There's a saying in the submarine world: "If you're cruising along and the ride gets rough, go deeper. Eventually it smooths out." Near the surface, waves can toss you around, but with the right tools and understanding, depth brings stability.

That mindset followed me into financial planning.

Submarines use many instruments to navigate, but the one most people recognize is the periscope. A periscope doesn't run the ship or make decisions—it provides perspective. It allows you to briefly lift your view above the surface, understand your surroundings, and choose a deliberate direction.

That's the thinking behind the Retirement Periscope™.

Good financial planning doesn't require constant vigilance or technical obsession. It requires the ability to periodically step back, see the full picture, and understand how your decisions fit together. When you have that perspective, fear diminishes and confidence grows.

Your Personal CFO

Over the years, my role has evolved into what I often describe as a personal chief financial officer (CFO). Most people think of a CFO as someone who manages money, but a good one manages systems. They make sure all the moving parts work together, risks are identified early, and decisions support long-term goals.

That's how I approach planning for the families I work with.

As I'm far more comfortable talking than writing, my goal is for this book to sound like a conversation, with plain language, clear explanations, and no unnecessary complexity. My goal isn't to impress you with jargon; it's to help you understand what matters and why. To give you clarity, reduce fear, and empower action. To help you gain a better understanding of how the multiple pieces of the retirement puzzle fit together—income, investments, insurance, taxes, and legacy—so you can make decisions with intention instead of guesswork.

Who This Book Is For

This book is written for real people with real questions. It's not aimed exclusively at high-net-worth families or financial insiders. In my practice, I've long believed that about 20 percent of the people who come to us can't afford to work with us, and we help them anyway. I trust God to send the other 80 percent who meet our needs, and He's been faithful. That philosophy has shaped how I work and why I do what I do.

My priority has always been simple and serious: making sure you don't outlive your money.

I consider this work a calling, not just a gig. If my only motivation were maximizing profit, I'd run my business very differently. Instead I focus on helping people sleep better at night. Our company slogan is "Your key to stress-free," and I mean that. If your financial plan is keeping you awake, something needs adjusting.

To be clear, this book is not a get-rich-quick guide. It's not a lecture on complex investment theory, and it's not about chasing the highest returns. Retirement planning isn't a competition—it's about durability. It's about preparing, coordinating, and making sure your money supports your life for as long as you need it.

Looking Ahead

Whether you're nearing retirement or still have time on your side, gaining perspective now can make a meaningful difference later. You don't need to have everything figured out, and you don't need to become an expert in finance to move forward with confidence. What matters is understanding how the major pieces of your financial life connect and recognizing when a decision in one area affects something else down the line.

As you read through this book, my goal is to help you see those connections more clearly. We'll step back together and look at retirement planning as a system, not a collection of unrelated choices. You'll begin to understand why certain questions deserve more attention, why some risks are worth addressing sooner rather than later, and why preparation almost always beats reaction.

This isn't about predicting the future or locking yourself into a rigid plan. Life changes. Markets change. Families change. A good plan is designed with these realities in mind. It's flexible, it's coordinated, and it's built to adapt as conditions shift. When you understand how the system works, those adjustments feel manageable instead of overwhelming.

The purpose of the Retirement Periscope is to give you that steady vantage point—a way to periodically lift your view, check your bearings, and move forward deliberately. With clarity comes confidence. With confidence comes the ability to act rather than worry.

That's what this book is here to help you do.

SECTION ONE

THE MAN BEHIND THE PERISCOPE

CHAPTER 1

A

SUBMARINER'S VISION

I was only eight years old when I decided I wanted to work in submarines when I grew up. Honestly, I couldn't tell you why. Most third-grade boys I knew wanted to be race car drivers, firemen, or cowboys. Some wanted to be astronauts and explore space—NASA was gearing up for the Gemini program in 1964. Not me. I wanted to go to the bottom of the sea.

Unlike many of those would-be A. J. Foyts and John Glenns, I actually stuck to my boyhood vision. Even as a youngster, I had a problem-solving mindset. And I knew that if I wanted to work on submarines, I'd have to join the US Navy.

It wasn't surprising that I gravitated toward the military. My dad was a career US Marine serving thirty-one years (including time as a drill instructor). Mom had also been in the Marine Corps, driving a truck during World War II.

As you might imagine, I couldn't get away with *anything* as a kid.

Anchors Aweigh

After high school, I headed to the US Naval Academy. Annapolis was beautiful, but make no mistake—it was also four years of pressure and purpose. From the moment I reported, I learned that everything had to be earned: every privilege, every bit of free time, even every minute of sleep. We were taught that discipline wasn't punishment; it was preparation.

I majored in electrical engineering, which fit right into that problem-solving mindset I mentioned. Engineering involves combining parts that don't seem to fit and making them work. We learned to think in systems. Every wire, every circuit, and every valve connects to something else. That systems thinking became the foundation of how I approach both engineering and financial planning.

Graduation meant more than a diploma; it meant orders. Mine pointed straight toward the Navy's nuclear submarine program. Nuclear power is one of the most demanding specialties in the military. Before we even boarded a boat, we completed nuclear power school. It took months of studying physics, chemistry, thermodynamics, and reactor theory. The instructors were brilliant and relentless. A single missed calculation could have real-world consequences, so accuracy became second nature.

Life Beneath the Waves

When I finally earned my place aboard a submarine, it felt like stepping into another world. Submarines are not large ships, just long steel tubes filled with machinery and people. Everything hums, rattles, and smells faintly of oil and metal. You sleep in racks stacked three high. Often you're next to torpedoes or piping that can feel warmer than your blanket. Privacy is pretty much nonexistent, except maybe in your dreams.

That environment teaches humility and respect in a hurry. Everyone has a job, and every job matters. The youngest sailor in the engine room can bring the entire operation to a halt with a single oversight, so we double-checked everything. Then we checked it again. If a gauge looked even slightly off, we didn't guess—we verified. "Trust but verify" is still one of my guiding philosophies.

There's no running from trouble underwater. You can't pull over, call for help, or get a tow. You solve the problem where you are, with the tools you have, alongside the people you trust. That kind of pressure either breaks you or builds you.

Qualifying as a submarine officer was one of the proudest moments of my life. Later, earning the title of qualified chief engineer felt like achieving my third-grade dream. It wasn't a title handed out lightly. The qualification enabled me to run the nuclear propulsion plant, where I handled power generation and life support systems. These systems made sure our crew could breathe. The process took many hours of study, practice drills, and oral boards, then testing by senior engineers. I had to explain every pipe and pump without looking. When that final signature went into my qualification book, I felt ten feet tall.

Pressure, Planning, and Perspective

Submarine duty is an education in risk management. Before every dive, we went over checklists that seemed endless. Every valve had to be in the right position, every backup tested. We planned for things we hoped would never happen: flooding, fires, power loss. And when we weren't at sea, we drilled. Emergencies, navigation, damage control—you name it, we practiced it. Repetition wasn't glamorous, but it saved lives.

Life aboard was also about trust. You can't fake competence when you're sealed in a steel tube hundreds of feet below the surface. The crew learns quickly who can be counted on. Leadership isn't about barking orders but about earning confidence. I found that listening often carried more weight than speaking. When someone knows you value their input, they'll give you their best effort.

Lessons in Leadership (and Life Insurance)

During those deployments, I discovered that leadership also means stewardship. Junior sailors looked to officers not just for orders but for guidance. Some were barely out of high school, far from home, with steady paychecks for the first time in their lives. They asked questions about taxes, car loans, even life insurance. I realized many of them were getting bad advice from smooth-talking salesmen on the pier. That didn't sit right with me.

I began hosting informal talks in my free time. I covered the basics: how interest operates, what an insurance policy entails, and the importance of budgeting. I didn't plan to become a financial advisor; I just wanted to help my people stay out of trouble. That's what good leaders do.

Those conversations planted a seed. I began studying more about personal finance on my own time. If I was going to give advice, I wanted it to be correct. I earned my insurance and securities licenses with A. L. Williams, now called Primerica. My goal wasn't to make money. I just wanted to understand the system. This way, I could protect my sailors from being taken advantage of.

One incident sticks with me: A young sailor was about to buy a whole life insurance policy that would've eaten up most of his paycheck. He didn't need it; he just needed term coverage to protect his family while he built savings. I sat down with him and went through the numbers line by line. When he realized how much he was going to overpay, he tore up the paperwork on the spot. Moments like that showed me how a little honest information can change someone's path.

Meanwhile, my Navy career continued to evolve. I worked as an instructor at the Naval Submarine School, training the next generation. Teaching helped me simplify complex ideas into plain language. This skill later became useful for explaining finances to clients. After about ten years of active duty, I faced a tough choice. The Navy wanted to send me on back-to-back sea tours. I loved the service, but I also loved my family. Long deployments would've meant missing too many moments at home. I decided to transfer to the reserves, where I could continue serving while finding a new balance.

I spent my last eight years as an engineering duty officer. This small, specialized group handles the technical oversight of major Navy projects. We handled everything from research labs to large-scale acquisition programs. The work demanded the same attention to detail I'd learned under the ocean, only now applied on land. I often joke that I'm a "recovering engineer," but truth be told, that mindset never really leaves you.

The View Through a Different Periscope

I spent a total of twenty years in service—twelve in submarines and eight as an engineering duty officer. I retired proud, grateful, and wiser than the day I'd walked into Annapolis. The Navy gave me more than a career; it gave me a way of thinking. I learned that every complex problem can be solved by gathering facts, testing assumptions, and acting with integrity.

That principle carried me into my second act. Managing a nuclear reactor and analyzing a client's finances are alike. You must first understand the system, then identify the risks, and finally, plan for every possible outcome. My time beneath the sea didn't just teach me how to manage machines—it taught me how to manage uncertainty. If there's one lesson I've carried from those days underwater, it's this: Preparation beats panic every time. On a submarine, you plan for every possibility because you don't get second chances, and financial life works the same way. The surface may look calm, but unseen currents can shift everything. The best way to face them is with a clear outlook, steady guidance, and a plan that accounts for what you can't see coming.

That philosophy, shaped by pressure and experience, became the core of my career after the Navy. But at the time, I didn't know where it would lead. All I knew was that I had a knack for solving puzzles and a heart for helping people who couldn't always help themselves.

And it all started with that eight-year-old boy who wanted to go to the bottom of the sea.

CHAPTER 2

LIFE ABOVE WATER

When I left active service, I didn't sail straight into finance—I surfaced gradually. After twenty years in the Navy, I wanted structure, so I took a defense contracting job. It kept me close to what I knew: flowcharts, checklists, and mission logs. The projects were large and the work precise, but something was missing. I wasn't solving human problems, just technical ones.

Even then, the phone kept ringing. Former shipmates would call asking about taxes, insurance, or what to do with a new 401(k). They trusted me because I had once helped them figure out what really mattered in a life insurance policy. Before long, I was spending more time explaining compound interest than combustion cycles. I discovered that the mindset used to run a submarine reactor—analyze, verify, act—can also help families keep their finances afloat.

From Circuits to Spreadsheets

I began by helping relatives and friends "on the side." Nights and weekends turned into short courses in budgeting, investment basics, and risk management. I never planned to change careers; I simply wanted to keep people from being taken advantage of. But one question led to another, and pretty soon I was hooked.

By the late 1990s, I was working full-time in defense contracting and part-time as a fledgling financial planner. In 2002, that balance finally shifted. I set up my first firm—what would become Outlook Financial Center—while still clocking in with my contractor badge during the day. In truth, I thought I was building a hobby. God had other ideas.

My first clients were mostly sailors, neighbors, and church friends. They wanted straight answers, not sales pitches. They came in worried about how to pay off debt, buy insurance, or save for college. I listened, ran the numbers, and gave them a path forward. Their relief was contagious. Helping people sleep better at night felt a lot better than keeping a software system bug-free.

Word spread slowly but steadily. Each family I helped told another, and soon weekends felt too short. My home office looked like mission control. Forms were stacked like sonar logs, and calculators took the place of old torpedo manuals. Clients soon started asking, "You do everything for us except our taxes—why not that too?" They had a point.

Years earlier, when I was still in the Navy, I had taken a tax preparation course offered by a well-known national company, not because I planned to make a career out of it but because I wanted to understand my own returns. I figured if I could navigate a nuclear reactor manual, I ought to be able to decode the IRS instructions. I threw myself into the coursework, determined to master every form and schedule. When the final exam results came back, I had earned the second-highest score in the entire country.

That knowledge became crucial when I saw how taxes and financial planning are connected. In 2008, I started Assurance Tax & Business Services. It was another part of the puzzle that completed the vision for Outlook Financial Center.

Around the same time, I saw that clients also needed help managing investments in a more direct and transparent way. Many firms sell products. I wanted something different—an advisory arm. Here, we could be true fiduciaries. We would recommend what truly serves the client. That's how Wellness Investment Advisors came to life.

The name wasn't accidental. Financial health is a lot like physical health—you can't just treat one symptom. You have to look at the entire system. Wellness Investment Advisors is the registered investment advisor (RIA) branch of the business. They help clients develop and maintain portfolios that fit their overall plans, instead of the opposite.

My engineering background also shaped the way I approached investing. I had spent years studying how every valve and circuit in a submarine worked together to keep the vessel stable. Investing, to me, followed the same logic.

You analyze the system, identify potential weak points, and design layers of protection. You don't guess—you test, verify, and plan for contingencies. We focus on real results instead of flashy returns. Our goals are maintaining steady growth, managing risk, and sticking to the plan, even when the market gets tough.

By 2010, the structure was complete. I was officially running three complementary entities:

1. **Outlook Financial Center**—a comprehensive planning and insurance solutions firm

2. **Wellness Investment Advisors**—an RIA firm for investments and wealth management

3. **Assurance Tax & Business Services**—a tax preparation and year-round planning firm

Each part has its own role, but together they act like compartments in a single vessel. They are sealed yet connected, working in harmony to help families through any financial challenge.

That was also the year I finally cut the cord, leaving corporate life to go full-time in financial planning. I've never looked back.

From One Man's Desk to a Team Effort

Growth brought new challenges. What began as one guy with a desk, a calculator, and a vision quickly turned into a coordinated effort requiring systems, people, and trust. I had to learn to delegate—to build a team that shared my values and could carry the same steady approach that had guided me beneath the waves.

Each of our three entities plays a different role, but none works in isolation. A tax decision can affect an investment choice, which in turn can shape a family's insurance needs. It's all connected, just like the systems of a submarine. I want our team to think that way: not as three separate departments but as one crew working from a common set of charts.

Over time, that mindset paid off. Today, Outlook Financial Center manages around $30 million in assets. This is a big jump from about $6 million just a few years ago. Our reach now goes beyond Ohio, serving clients across the country and even overseas. We may be small by Wall Street standards, but that's fine by me. I'd rather run a tight, well-trained crew than a massive ship that can't turn on a dime.

A huge part of that success is family. My wife, Cheryl, and I have a blended family with eight kids. Her daughter Lori, my stepdaughter, has worked in the business for over ten years. After her husband passed away, she felt the deep heartache and confusion that comes when finances are not managed well. Her son's inheritance was tied up by the state, and that ordeal lit a fire in her to make sure other families never went through the same thing. She studied hard and earned her licenses, then took on more responsibility. Eventually she became the operational heart of the company. Truth be told, she's better at the day-to-day than I am.

My long-term goal is for Lori to fully take over. I will remain for mentorship and to help with complex cases. When that day comes, I hope no one notices a change—that's the mark of a solid system. I never wanted a business built around my name; I wanted an entity with integrity, a steady ship that keeps its heading no matter who's in command.

That's why I chose the name Outlook Financial Center instead of Burnette & Associates. A clear outlook matters more than any single person. If the company runs smoothly after I've stepped away, that will be my proudest accomplishment.

A Calling, Not a Gig

Some people see finance as a competition. They aim to close the biggest deals, manage the largest portfolios, or build the flashiest offices. Those were never my goals. I wanted to earn a comfortable living, but the real reward is in making an impact. It feels great to see a widow breathe easier after sorting out her benefits. It's also rewarding to watch a couple realize they can retire with dignity, free from worry about burdening their children.

In many ways, financial planning turned out to be ministry work disguised as math. Every client who walks through our door is carrying something heavier than numbers—a worry, a regret, or a dream they're afraid to name. My job is to listen first, then design a plan that brings peace. If the Navy taught me that preparation beats panic every time, life taught me that faith fills the gap when numbers fall short.

That calling eventually shaped not just how I worked but where I chose to put down roots.

Anchored in Troy, Ohio

When Cheryl decided it was time to move back home to Ohio, she simply said, "I'm going—are you coming?" I didn't hesitate. We settled in Piqua, a small community that suits us perfectly. It's close enough to clients around Dayton and Troy, yet grounded in Midwestern values: faith, family, and follow-through. We planted the business in Troy. From there, Outlook Financial Center grew from a two-person office into a family-run operation with deep local roots and a global reach.

Even as technology lets us meet clients from coast to coast, I never want to lose that neighborly feel. Community involvement, like sponsoring a youth softball team or volunteering at county fairs, helps us stay connected to what matters: people. Helping others succeed isn't just good business; it's good stewardship.

Looking Ahead

Today, when I look through the periscope of retirement planning, I see parallels to those long days underwater. A good financial plan, like a good dive plan, demands discipline, redundancy, and trust. You account for what can go wrong before you ever leave port. You stay calm when the alarms sound. And you remember that success depends on the whole crew, not the captain alone.

That's the spirit behind Outlook Financial Center—three integrated entities, one mission: to help ordinary families navigate uncertain waters and make sure their money outlives them. The systems have changed since my Navy days, but the principle remains the same: preparation, teamwork, and faith keep you afloat.

Next, I'll share why I focus on the people I do and what separates real planning from the cookie-cutter kind that leaves too many drifting without direction.

CHAPTER 3

REAL PLANNING FOR REAL PEOPLE

Turn on the TV any weekend and you'll see the same financial commercials over and over—smiling couples clinking wineglasses on a yacht, grandchildren running through beach houses, golfers high-fiving on private greens. The music swells, a calm voice talks about "building a legacy," and you already know who they're talking to.

They're not speaking to the teacher checking prices in the grocery aisle or the factory worker figuring out when he can afford to retire. They're speaking to the folks who already have wealth, the people with private bankers and trust attorneys on speed dial. The ads never say it outright, but the message is clear: This isn't for you unless you already have money.

My philosophy's a bit different.

Serving the People Who Keep Things Running

From day one, I made a conscious choice to serve real people, not just high-net-worth investors. Most of our clients are middle-income families: teachers, small business owners, farmers, and factory workers. They're the same kind of people I served beside in uniform, and they deserve honest guidance just as much as anyone sitting on Wall Street.

That choice went against common advice in my profession. The industry tells you to chase assets under management as a metric of success, meaning the more money a client already has, the more you make. Many advisors won't even take a meeting unless someone has half a million to invest. To me, that never made sense. I wasn't called to this work to help the rich get richer. I'm here to make sure your money lasts longer than you do.

When someone walks into my office, I don't start by asking how much they have. I start by asking what keeps them up at night. I believe God puts people in front of me for a reason—some come with wealth, some come with worries, but all deserve to be treated with respect. As I told you at the outset, about 20 percent of the people who come to us can't afford us. I trust God to send the other 80 percent to meet our needs, and He's never failed.

Planning vs. Advising

Too many advisors look only at numbers. I look at stories. You can tell me a person's income, but that doesn't explain why they're still paying off credit cards or why they haven't updated their will. Real planning requires more than math—it requires empathy.

I tell people all the time: I'm a financial planner, not a financial advisor. The difference may sound small, but it's everything. Advisors often focus on investments—how to chase returns or move money around. Planners focus on people—how to build a complete system that actually works. My job is to look at the whole picture, including income, debt, insurance, taxes, and goals, and then figure out how all the valves and gauges fit together. That's where the engineering brain comes in handy.

In our business, there are really three main kinds of professionals who can give you financial advice, depending on their license. You've got insurance agents, who represent insurance companies; registered representatives, who work for broker-dealers; and investment advisor representatives, who work for registered investment advisory (RIA) firms.

Here's the key difference: those first two professionals technically work for the company, not the client. They're paid by commissions from the products they sell. Most are good, honest people, but legally they're only required to meet a suitability standard. In other words, what they recommend just has to fit your profile—it doesn't have to be the best or most cost-effective choice for you.

Investment advisor representatives, on the other hand, are bound by the fiduciary standard. That means we have to put the client's interest ahead of our own at all times. No exceptions. That's the lane I work in, and it's where I'm most comfortable. It aligns with how I was trained in the Navy—follow the code, protect your crew, and do what's right even when nobody's watching.

Some folks in the industry hold both licenses. There's nothing illegal about that, but it can get confusing. One moment they're acting as fiduciaries, and the next they're selling products under the suitability rule. To me, that's like switching submarine captains mid-dive. You may surface safely, or you may not—but why take the chance?

That's why I chose to build Outlook Financial Center around the planning model. We don't lead with products; we lead with purpose. We don't sell for commissions; we serve for results. Real financial planning is about creating clarity, not confusion.

Faith Over Finances

My guiding principle is simple: If I take care of people and do it right, the money will follow.

That belief has never failed me. There were times, especially in the early days, when I didn't know where the next client was coming from. But then a door would open—a referral from a friend, a pastor, or a grateful family we had helped years before. I've seen that pattern repeat so often, it's hard not to believe it's by design. When you focus on doing what's right, the business takes care of itself.

Many of our tax clients—close to a third—are pastors and missionaries serving around the world. Their financial lives can be complex if they work overseas, with special tax rules and unique income situations that typical tax software can't handle. Helping them navigate those details isn't just technical work—it's personal. It's about freeing them to focus on the work they were called to do.

That same spirit guides how we serve everyone who walks through our doors. I still remember one couple who came in years ago, drowning in debt. They were scared and embarrassed, afraid to even open their statements. Most firms would've turned them away because they weren't "profitable." We took them on anyway. It didn't happen overnight, but together we built a plan that worked. They're debt-free now, saving for retirement, and teaching their kids to start early. They've referred more families to us than any marketing campaign ever could.

And then there was the woman who came to us after a divorce that left her finances in ruins. Her ex-husband had filed for bankruptcy, and she got pulled into it. By the time she found us, her confidence was gone. We built her a plan from the ground up: paid off her bills, rebuilt her budget, and helped her see a clear path forward. Over time she told me she finally felt a sense of peace about money she had never had before. Now, when she stops by the office, she's always smiling. She's thriving in her career and has become one of our greatest advocates.

These types of clients are walking billboards for what happens when planning is done right. Watching that kind of change happen is what makes me want to come to work every morning.

Beyond the Office

That same belief in steady progress carries into our community work. I support programs like 4-H and FFA because they teach young people what every good plan requires—discipline, patience, and pride in a job well done.

At the county fair each summer, I watch kids explain how they budgeted for feed and supplies or how they stuck with a project even when it was hard. Those lessons stay with them long after the ribbons fade. They're learning how effort turns into results, just like our clients do when they stick with a plan.

We also stay involved with local schools, veterans' groups, and small business programs. I see this work as an extension of our mission. The same people who trust us with their finances are the ones teaching, mentoring, and running the businesses that hold our community together. When they thrive, everyone does.

We also serve our community by sharing our expertise with TV and online audiences. Lori and I often appear on local news stations in Cleveland, Columbus, and Dayton to talk about financial planning. These segments give us a chance to reach people who might never walk through our door and to break down complex topics in plain language. That's always been the goal—helping normal, everyday people make sense of their money, wherever they are.

Steady Course, Clear Purpose

Markets rise and fall. Rules change. Headlines come and go. Through it all, I try to keep my clients focused on what doesn't move—integrity, discipline, and patience. When turbulence hits, I remind them of a submariner's truth: Sometimes you go deeper to find calm water.

Financial planning works the same way. The surface can get noisy, but the deeper you go into a sound plan, the steadier things feel. It's not about predicting the future; it's about preparing for it with confidence.

That's what "real planning for real people" means to me. It's not a slogan—it's a commitment to clarity over complexity and people over products. When a client leaves my office relaxed for the first time in years, that's success.

Helping people find that steady course is why I do this. It's the purpose behind every plan and the proof that doing good work still matters.

CHAPTER 4

THE PROBLEM WITH PLANNING

Why People Avoid Financial Planning—
and Why They Shouldn't

It isn't just those TV commercials we talked about in the last chapter that make most folks shy away from the topic of financial planning. The reasons for this disconnect are largely related to perception and a lack of understanding. Because, let's face it, you don't know what you don't know.

In this chapter, we'll look at why so many people steer clear of financial planning and why that hesitation can be costly. We'll also set the stage for what's coming later in the book, where we'll dive deeper into many of these topics—like investments, insurance, taxes, and legacy planning—and show how they all connect below the surface to form a complete financial picture.

Why People Avoid Planning

On a submarine, you can't look out the windshield to see what's ahead. You trust your instruments, the crew, and the plan. But imagine trying to run silent and deep with no map, no bearings, and no idea what lies in front of you. That's how most people handle their money. They stay submerged in the day-to-day, convinced that if they just keep cruising, everything will work out. Until they hit something they never saw coming.

For many, financial planning feels just as intimidating as navigating underwater without sonar. The concepts can be complex and the language confusing. Add in bad experiences or mistrust of the financial industry, and it's easy to see why people would rather avoid the whole topic. Some think they don't have enough money to "qualify" for professional help. Others believe financial planning is only for retirees or for people with million-dollar portfolios. Still others just feel uneasy opening up about money at all—it's been an undiscussed subject in many households for generations.

Then there's another common problem: fragmentation. People will go to a tax preparer when it's time to file, an insurance agent when they need coverage, or an estate attorney when they're writing a will. Each of those professionals may do good work—but they're often working in isolation, focused on their own station without seeing the whole vessel. It's like having a submarine crew with each department working hard but none of them talking to the others. The navigator might be plotting one course while the engineer is managing power in another direction. Without coordination, the sub drifts. Your financial life works the same way: taxes, insurance, investments, and estate planning all affect one another, and if they're not aligned, you can find yourself off course before you realize it.

Most of the time, the problem isn't that people make bad choices. It's that they make uninformed ones—without anyone overseeing how all the moving parts fit together.

Why Cookie-Cutter Advice Fails

In the submarine world, every vessel is different, with different depth ratings, crew experience, and mission objectives. You can't take a checklist from one sub and expect it to fit another perfectly. Financial planning works the same way. What works for one family may not work for another, and yet the financial industry still churns out cookie-cutter advice as if everyone's life follows the same schematic.

As we discussed in the previous chapter, that's exactly what most of those glossy commercials are selling: prepackaged strategies designed for people who already have wealth. They're built for the smoothest seas, not for real life. But most folks don't have trust funds or corporate pensions—they have paychecks, mortgages, kids, aging parents, and unexpected expenses that pop up when they can least afford them. A plan that ignores those realities isn't a plan at all. It's a brochure.

Too many advisors focus narrowly on investments and ignore everything else that affects a client's financial life. They talk in percentages and projections, not people and priorities. Again, I'm not necessarily knocking them for that. They're often good people just doing their jobs and following a formula, and, for many of their clients, they're providing a valuable service.

The people I serve just don't happen to be that type of client.

The truth is life doesn't fit neatly into a formula. No spreadsheet or algorithm can tell you how to plan for the loss of a spouse, a medical diagnosis, or a child returning home after college. Those are real human moments that require judgment, flexibility, and compassion, which are traits you won't find in a templated plan or a quarterly performance report.

That's why I built Outlook Financial Center around planning, not product-pushing. Real planning accounts for every valve, gauge, and subsystem working together, just like a well-trained crew. It's not about squeezing everyone into the same model but about building the right model for *you*.

You Don't Know What You Don't Know

Like I told you at the beginning of this chapter, most of the anxiety and uncertainty surrounding financial planning stems from those seven words.

Most folks don't know just how much they don't know until it's too late. They assume that because they've filed their taxes, started a 401(k), or bought life insurance, they've "got things covered." But financial planning isn't a list of one-time tasks; it's a connected system in which each decision affects the next.

Most people don't know that the age when you start collecting Social Security can affect far more than just the size of your check. You may know waiting increases your monthly benefit, but you might not realize how that choice ties into your taxes, your spouse's future income, and even your overall retirement strategy.

Did you know that if you don't have an estate plan, the government already has one for you? Most don't. And did you know that your will isn't necessarily the final word in who inherits what?

Most folks don't realize how closely their investments, insurance, taxes, and income plans are intertwined. You can't just fix one piece and ignore the others any more than a submarine could run safely if the engine crew never talked to navigation. Each part has to work in coordination or the whole system drifts off course.

That's where real planning makes all the difference. You don't have to know everything; you just need someone who understands how all the parts connect. I often tell clients to think of me as their personal chief financial officer, someone who lays out the options, explains the trade-offs, and helps them decide which course makes the most sense. (We'll talk more about that in the next chapter.)

I once helped a client who needed about $300,000 from his individual retirement account (IRA) to build a new home. Most people would have taken it all at once, thinking that was the only option. Instead, we split the withdrawal over two years—enough to fund each construction milestone while keeping him in a lower tax bracket. That single adjustment saved him roughly $37,000 in income tax and allowed the remaining balance to keep growing until it was needed.

That's what comprehensive planning is all about—seeing the whole picture and finding smarter ways to reach your goals. Once you start seeing that bigger picture, the fog begins to lift, and the fear goes with it.

Financial planning isn't about chasing returns or predicting the market. It's about engineering a system that can withstand whatever comes. As I learned in the Navy, if you build with foresight and discipline, the system holds.

What Does a Sound Financial Plan Look Like?

That's really a trick question, of course. The best financial plan is tailored specifically to your unique situation—we've already learned that cookie-cutter plans don't work. So the best answer doesn't describe what a good plan *looks like* but what a good plan *does*:

1. **It builds durability.** It ensures your money lasts longer than you do. Without it, too many retirees end up greeting people at Walmart or asking, "Would you like fries with that?" because their savings ran out.

2. **It prevents costly mistakes.** A proper plan coordinates taxes, insurance, investments, and estate documents so that every part works in harmony. It anticipates pitfalls like long-term care costs or withdrawal penalties before they become problems.

3. **It provides peace of mind.** This one's *huge*. Once people finally see their full financial picture, the anxiety disappears. They understand the "why" behind the strategy, and they can sleep at night knowing there's a system in place.

That's what we mean when we talk about a comprehensive approach. You don't need to be wealthy to deserve it—you just need to be willing to look through the periscope and face what's really there.

Bringing It All Together

Planning isn't about perfection. It's about progress, preparation, and perspective. The families I serve aren't chasing yachts or country clubs—they're chasing peace of mind.

When they understand their plan, they stop reacting and start leading. And that's when everything changes.

You can't control the waves, but you can control your depth, your direction, and your readiness. That's true in a submarine, and it's true in life.

CHAPTER 5

THE OUTLOOK APPROACH

When I was still in the Navy, spending my downtime helping sailors with their finances, I noticed how differently people approached money compared with how we handled systems aboard a submarine. As we touched on in the last chapter, most regular working folks manage their finances one piece at a time—taxes here, investments there—without realizing how closely those parts affect each other. What my years underwater taught me was the opposite: Every valve, circuit, and checklist had to align to keep the mission safe.

That mindset of engineering, verifying, and anticipating is the backbone of my approach to financial planning. Rather than patching problems as they appear, we design a system that already knows how its parts fit together. It's planning that behaves like a well-tuned reactor: precise, disciplined, and built to handle pressure.

The idea isn't complicated, but it's rare. Most people have bits and pieces of their financial system handled by different professionals who rarely communicate. It's like a submarine crew with the navigator plotting one course while the engineer adjusts power in another direction. Without coordination, you drift.

Our approach avoids that trap, and we never use a cookie-cutter plan. No two clients share the same goals, timelines, or risk tolerance, so we don't force them into a premade mold. A good plan should fit your life the way a pressure hull fits its depth rating: engineered to your exact specifications, tested for integrity, and flexible enough to handle change. Templates might save time, but they ignore nuance, and in finance, nuance is what keeps the whole vessel safe.

That's why our approach emphasizes customization, communication, and control. It's about building systems that hold up under real-world conditions, not just theoretical ones.

Engineering Over Guesswork

In the Navy, guessing wasn't an option. If a gauge looked wrong, you didn't hope it would fix itself. You traced the cause, verified the numbers, and logged the correction. That same habit defines the way we work with clients today.

Every family who walks through our doors presents a new puzzle to solve. We start by understanding the whole picture—their goals, resources, and blind spots—and then trace how money moves through their system. Where is pressure building? Where is something leaking? Where can we reroute to keep things stable and efficient?

That process is what sets our planning apart. We don't deal in theory; we deal in results. My background and training as a Master Registered Financial Consultant (MRFC) gave me the tools to bridge numbers and reality, to take complex, technical material and turn it into real-world solutions that make sense.

Clients don't want jargon. They want clarity. That means every recommendation we make has to pass a simple test:

1. Can it be explained plainly?

2. Can it be justified mathematically?

3. Does it actually make life better for the person sitting across from us?

That's what practical financial planning looks like—less theory, more function. Before I ever show a client a portfolio, product, or strategy, I take it apart. I want to understand every component. I want to know how it's built, how it reacts under stress, and what could go wrong if conditions change. If I can't explain it clearly and confidently, it doesn't make the cut.

That discipline comes from years of engineering systems in which precision mattered. In finance, the stakes are different, but the principle is the same: A plan should function under pressure, not just when everything's calm.

My MRFC training reinforced that mindset. It's all about practical application, turning theory into solutions that work in the real world. That's how we approach planning: We test, verify, and simplify until every part fits together.

We also keep cost efficiency in mind. Our goal is to provide professional-grade strategies at a fair price, which means focusing on what works rather than what sells. We don't set high account minimums or chase only affluent clients. I believe solid planning should be accessible to anyone willing to engage in the process.

Our system is built on transparency and validation. When we recommend something, it's because it's been tested, reviewed, and proven to fit your goals, not because it pays more or fits a company's quota.

The Retirement Periscope™

Everything I've described, the coordination, engineering, and accountability, comes together in the Retirement Periscope, the framework we use to keep every client's plan on course.

The idea comes straight from my Navy days. A periscope lets you get a perspective above the surface without exposing the entire vessel, and our process does the same thing for your finances. We periodically "raise the scope" to see the whole picture—investments, income, insurance, taxes, and estate planning—and make sure everything still aligns with your goals. Through the periscope, we ask key questions:

- Are you still headed in the right direction?

- Have tax laws, markets, or life events shifted your landscape?

- Do we need to adjust course before something drifts off target?

It's not about predicting the future; it's about preparing for it. The periscope gives us visibility and control. Once you can see clearly, uncertainty loses its power.

Clients often tell me they feel lighter after this process, like they finally understand how all the pieces fit together. That clarity turns worry into confidence. Ultimately, the Retirement Periscope is how we put our approach into action, building and maintaining a coordinated plan that can handle whatever life brings because every part and every decision is connected.

The Power of Partnership

No plan works in isolation, and neither do we. The Power of Partnership is what keeps everything running within our office, across our network, and in the relationships we build with clients.

Our in-house team may be small, but it's efficient. Everyone knows their role and how their work supports the larger mission. We hold regular review meetings to make sure no detail is overlooked and no client goal drifts off course. I encourage honest conversation and fresh perspectives; in team discussions, the youngest member always speaks first, and I go last. It's a simple way to keep ideas genuine instead of filtered.

Beyond our walls, we collaborate with a network of trusted professionals—certified public accountants (CPAs), tax attorneys, insurance specialists, and others who share our values. I don't claim to know everything, but I do know where to find the right answers fast. Whether it's confirming a tax rule or double-checking an insurance detail, clients see that process firsthand, and it gives them confidence that their plan is built on facts, not assumptions.

This is where that personal chief financial officer (CFO) role I mentioned earlier really comes into play. Most people think of a CFO as the person who manages money. In reality, a good CFO manages *systems*. They set direction and vision—where the company wants to go—but they're also responsible for making sure the finances and operations support that vision. They manage cash flow, allocate resources, anticipate risks, and ensure that every department's decisions align with the company's financial reality.

That's what I do for the families I serve. I coordinate the moving parts: the taxes, the investments, the insurance, and the income planning. I analyze how each decision affects the others, then translate the technical details into clear choices. I don't just hand you a plan and walk away; I help you understand the strategy behind it so you can make confident, informed decisions.

A true CFO doesn't just track numbers. They anticipate what's next, adjust when conditions change, and keep the system stable through uncertainty. That's exactly how we approach your financial life. We manage the flow, keep the systems balanced, and make sure your plan performs as designed. When you have that kind of coordination, you can stop worrying about what you might be missing and focus on the life you're building.

Our family is part of that partnership too. As I've told you, my stepdaughter Lori has been an essential part of our operation for more than a decade. She brings experience, empathy, and the kind of discipline that comes from years of doing this the right way. Her daughter Ashton and stepdaughter Jenna represent the next generation—tech-savvy, curious, and passionate about helping families see that financial planning doesn't have to be intimidating.

That multigenerational perspective is one of our greatest strengths. It gives our team a wider lens—experience that understands where clients have been and fresh insight into how the next generation thinks, spends, and plans. In our meetings, I always have the youngest person speak first, which keeps ideas honest and unvarnished and ensures I don't steer the conversation before everyone's had their say. That exchange of perspectives helps us build plans that resonate with every stage of life, from building a foundation to protecting a legacy.

The Power of Partnership extends beyond titles or credentials. It's about people working together—professionals, family, and clients—each contributing their expertise toward one shared goal: helping your money last longer than you do and giving you the confidence to enjoy life along the way.

Looking Ahead

Now that you've seen how our system works, from its engineering roots to the teamwork and accountability that keep it running, it's time to shift our focus forward. The next stage is all about perspective—what you need to know to chart the right course. We'll lift the periscope a little higher and take a clearer look at the key elements that shape retirement success: income, investments, insurance, taxes, and legacy.

You don't need to master every technical detail to stay on course. But understanding how these areas function and how to recognize warning signs before they become problems can make all the difference. When you know what matters and why, you can steer with confidence and avoid costly missteps.

Planning isn't about predicting what's ahead; it's about being prepared for whatever shows up on the radar. Preparation always beats panic, and a clear outlook always keeps you afloat.

STRATEGY THROUGH THE PERISCOPE

What You Need to Know to Chart the Right Course

CHAPTER 6

WHERE WILL THE MONEY COME FROM?

Retirement Income Planning

Your relationship with money changes as you progress through life. When you're young, your income is about survival—keeping a roof over your head, paying for bills, maybe raising a family. As time goes on and life gets more stable, the picture widens. You start thinking beyond the next paycheck. You build savings. You put money in a retirement account. You begin to connect your decisions with the kind of life you want later.

But throughout your entire working life, the pattern is the same: Money comes in from your job, and you save some of it when you can. As time goes on and your income grows, you might start looking for better things to do with your expendable income. That's how most people move through their career.

Retirement completely upends the landscape. You've moved from the accumulation phase to the distribution phase of your life, and it's a much bigger shift than most people expect. Suddenly the income isn't coming from your employer. Instead, it's coming from sources like Social Security, pensions, 401(k)s, and other retirement vehicles and investments. Each one has its own rules and its own purpose. But they all have one thing in common: on their own, they're almost never enough.

That's why understanding what each source does, and what it doesn't do, is so important. The goal isn't to pick one perfect source of income. It's to understand how all the pieces work together to support the life you want.

In this chapter, we'll walk through the basic building blocks of retirement income. We're not diving into strategy yet, just laying the groundwork so that when we do build your strategy, it rests on solid footing.

Social Security

For most of the families I work with, Social Security ends up being the cornerstone of their retirement income. You paid into it your entire working life, and now it pays you back—every month, like clockwork. It's steady, reliable, and adjusted for inflation. In plain English, it's a guaranteed income stream you've already earned.

I like to think of Social Security the same way I used to think about certain systems on the submarine: steady, dependable, and designed to keep running no matter what else is happening around you. It's not the flashiest part of the ship, but it's the part you trust.

A lot of people assume Social Security is simple: you hit a certain age, you file, and the check shows up. I wish it worked that way. The truth is, Social Security has more moving parts than most folks realize. The longer you wait to file—up to age seventy—the bigger your check gets. And that increase isn't small. The system grows your benefit by roughly 8 percent every year you delay. That can add up to a big difference over a long retirement.

But here's the part people sometimes overlook: Social Security isn't just about your income. It's also about your spouse's income too. Statistically, around 80 percent of women outlive their husbands, and often by several years. When one spouse passes, the surviving spouse keeps the larger of the two Social Security checks and loses the other one entirely. So the decision about when to take this benefit isn't just a timing issue—it's a long-term income issue that affects the survivor's lifestyle for the rest of their life.

There are also some surprises built into the system, both good and bad. I once worked with a client who started collecting his Social Security at age sixty-two, when he still had minor children at home (not a typical situation but more common than you might think). Those kids received benefits until they turned eighteen. He hadn't even known that was possible. Many folks don't.

And on the other end of the spectrum, I've seen people almost miss out on benefits completely. I once sat down with a teacher who had thirty-nine Social Security credits. The years you work are worth a certain number of credits, and you need forty to qualify for your own benefit. I told her, "Go get a part-time job—anything." She took a short-term job at a music store, earned her fortieth credit, and unlocked the benefit she would have lost forever.

Then there are situations that are just plain confusing. A widow I worked with was told by two separate Social Security offices that she could keep both her own check and her late husband's. She trusted that information—any of us would—but it turned out to be wrong, and she later received an overpayment notice for $8,800. Here's the really frustrating part, and this is important: The Social Security office cannot give advice. They're allowed only to give information about your record, not to tell you what you should do. So even though two offices told her the same thing, neither one was actually guiding her.

In the end, we helped her file an appeal, and the entire amount was forgiven, but it's a perfect example of why informed decision-making is so important.

The bottom line is this: Social Security is one of the strongest, most reliable systems on your retirement income submarine. But like anything else, it works best when you understand what it does, what it doesn't do, and how long you're likely to depend on it.

Pensions

If you're fortunate enough to have a pension, you've got something incredibly valuable: guaranteed income that lasts as long as you do. Pensions are becoming rare these days, but for those who have one, it's often one of the most important pieces of the retirement picture.

For many teachers, firefighters, police officers, and other public employees, their pension isn't just part of their plan—it *is* their plan. If they have any Social Security at all, it usually comes from part-time jobs they've held along the way (much like that teacher I just told you about).

Pensions come with their own rules: You'll choose between a single-life payout (higher monthly income but ends when you die) and a joint-life payout (lower income but continues for your spouse). You'll decide whether you want survivor benefits. And you may have the option to take a lump sum instead of monthly income. These choices have long-term consequences—not just for you but for your spouse if they depend on your income after you're gone.

A pension is a blessing, but it needs to be understood and coordinated with your other income sources, whatever those happen to be. Even without Social Security in the mix, your pension still has to blend with your savings, your investments, and everything else you've built for retirement.

Employer Retirement Plans and 401(k)s

For many folks, a 401(k) or a similar 403(b) or 457 is the backbone of their retirement savings. You put money in before taxes, it grows tax-deferred, and you pay taxes when you take it out in retirement. But there's more going on beneath the surface.

First, these plans come with required minimum distributions (RMDs) once you hit a certain age. Put simply, you have to withdraw money even if you don't need it. Those RMDs can affect your tax bill and your Medicare premiums. They also affect how long your money will last. You don't need to memorize the rules—that's what I'm here for—but you do need to know those rules exist.

Second, 401(k)s have unique flexibility if you retire at or after age fifty-five. There's an "age 55 rule" that lets you withdraw from your 401(k) without the 10 percent penalty if you leave your employer in the year you turn fifty-five or later. If you roll that money into an IRA right away, you lose that option.

And then there's the big one: beneficiary designations. In case you didn't know it (and don't feel bad—you're not alone), your beneficiary designation overrides your will.

I've reviewed 401(k)s for which the listed beneficiary was an ex-spouse, a deceased parent, or nobody at all. In one case, I caught an outdated beneficiary designation that would have sent over a million dollars to the wrong person. That's not a fun surprise for any family.

A 401(k) can be a great retirement income source, but only if you understand how the plan behaves once you retire.

IRAs and Roth IRAs

Individual retirement accounts (IRAs) are some of the most flexible tools you can have in retirement planning. They're not investments themselves—they're containers for your investments. A submarine isn't defined by the crew or even the mission. Those change. Rather, it's the vehicle that gets the crew where it needs to go. IRAs work the same way. The investments inside can change, but the "wrapper" determines the rules: how the money is taxed, when it can come out, and how it fits into your retirement income.

A traditional IRA is funded with pretax money. You get a tax break now, and you pay taxes later when you take the money out. Most people open traditional IRAs because they're easy to understand and because the tax deduction feels good in the year you make the contribution.

A Roth IRA works the opposite way. You pay the taxes up front, and in exchange, everything that grows inside that account—every dollar of interest, dividends, and long-term growth—can come out tax-free in retirement. That's a huge deal. If you're worried about tax rates going up or you just like the idea of having a bucket of money you can use without worrying about the IRS, a Roth IRA can be one of the most powerful tools you own.

Roth IRAs also don't have RMDs for the original owner, which means the IRS doesn't force you to take money out at a certain age. That extra control is often worth as much as the tax benefits.

And whether you have a traditional or a Roth IRA, the beneficiary form matters a lot. Whoever you list on that form gets the money, even if your will says something different. I've seen more trouble caused by an outdated IRA beneficiary than by almost any investment decision. Checking those forms takes five minutes and can save your family years of headaches.

The big idea here is simple: IRAs—traditional or Roth—give you flexibility, tax advantages, and control. They're not the strategy itself, but they're a solid part of the foundation your retirement strategy will eventually rest on.

Annuities

Annuities tend to get a bad rap these days, and honestly, a lot of that is because many people don't understand what they are or have only heard about the ones that weren't a good fit for somebody. At the end of the day, annuities are simply insurance products subject to the same stringent financial and underwriting oversight as any other insurance. And, like any insurance product, some are great, some are terrible, and some are just okay. That's not necessarily because they're faulty or fraudulent but because they're just not the right fit for your individual situation and goals. The key is being able to tell which is which.

Here's what surprises most folks about annuities: Social Security is an annuity. A pension is an annuity.

They're built on the exact same math, in which a big group of people pays into a system, and the people who live the longest are funded by the folks who don't. Modern annuities are based on the same actuarial science, and it's not a new idea. The concept goes all the way back to ancient Rome, when families of fallen soldiers received a lifetime payment in honor of their service. So annuities aren't some confusing new invention. They've been around for a thousand years.

What makes private annuities different from Social Security and pensions is how they're set up. Social Security is backed by the federal government, while pensions are backed by employers and run by huge actuarial systems. With a private annuity, *you* decide how much to put in and which features you want. The contract is then backed by an insurance company instead of by the government or your employer.

But the purpose of all of them is the same: guaranteed income you can't outlive.

Some annuities protect you from market losses. Some provide income that "rolls up" (grows) while you're waiting to turn it on, kind of like how Social Security grows the longer you delay your benefit. If someone tells me they want to start income in five or six years, for example, I look for an annuity with a strong roll-up rate during that waiting period. If someone has a longer time horizon, I might look at one with a different growth structure. The point is there's a wide range of designs, built for different timelines and goals.

And there are also annuities I avoid entirely (like variable, high-fee, commission-driven ones). I don't use those, not because they're inherently bad but because they're built for Wall Street, not for real people trying to make their income last.

Another thing to understand is how annuities interact with taxes. The "wrapper" around the annuity matters. An annuity inside an IRA has to follow RMD rules, but a Roth IRA annuity doesn't. Same product, different outcome—simply because of the wrapper it's inside.

And, finally, you have to be careful where you get advice. I've seen cases in which a bank's wealth manager drained a client's lifetime-income annuities just to satisfy her RMDs because draining the annuities didn't hurt the bank's fee-based accounts. It absolutely destroyed her guaranteed income. That's not a mistake; that's a business model. It's one of the reasons people get burned by annuities—not because the annuity was bad but because someone mishandled it.

Here's the simple truth: Annuities aren't good or bad. They're tools. Used correctly, they can provide lifetime income and peace of mind. Used incorrectly, they can make a mess.

But when you're trying to build a retirement income that will last as long as you do—especially through market ups and downs—an annuity can be one of the most valuable tools in the box.

Bringing It All Together

When you look at all the pieces of retirement income side by side, the bigger picture starts to come into sharper focus. Social Security (and/or a pension, if you have one) gives you a steady base. Your employer retirement plans and IRAs give you flexibility and control. Annuities can provide guaranteed income you can count on for life.

Each of these sources has its own job, but none of them are meant to carry the whole load by themselves. It's the way they work together that matters.

On a submarine, no single system keeps the boat running. You need propulsion, navigation, life support, electrical, hydraulics, and more, each doing their part. Lose one system, and you could still operate. Lose several, and things get a whole lot tougher. Retirement income works the same way. One source gives stability. Another gives flexibility. Another gives protection. Put them together, and you get something much stronger than any one piece could provide.

That's why understanding what your income sources are and what they're built to do is so important. Once you know their strengths, you can start to see how they support one another. And from there, you can build a retirement income plan that doesn't just look good on paper—it actually holds up over time.

CHAPTER 7

NAVIGATING SAFE INVESTMENTS

When you really think about it, much of life is about investments and dividends. You spend your career investing your time for dividends in the form of paychecks and benefits. You invest in Social Security or your pension, 401(k)s or other employer retirement programs, life insurance or annuities, all in exchange for guaranteed dividends once you're no longer earning a paycheck.

Of course, what separates these investments from what comes to mind when most people think of "investing" is that one little word: *guaranteed.* Most folks, or at least most of the folks I work with, think of "traditional" investing as a gamble. They think of Wall Street and the stock market.

Many don't want anything to do with it. Others are less hesitant but still cautious. To those in the latter group, I say, "You *should* be cautious." Wild, uniformed speculation can be kryptonite to your retirement. It's like diving in a sub without knowing the depth.

To those in the first group, who might view anything having to do with stocks and bonds as either out of their league or not worth the risk, I've got some news that might surprise you: You're probably already investing in the stock market.

Wall Street isn't some faraway world that concerns only day traders and TV pundits. If you've got a pension, a 401(k) or other retirement account (not including Social Security, which is totally government-subsidized), or any income-producing insurance product, you've got money in Wall Street. Those accounts don't grow beyond the principal all by themselves—they're tied to market indexes, mutual funds, or target-date funds that adjust automatically based on your age.

The point is, much of your financial life is already built on systems that rely on the market in one form or another. And whether or not you ever actually have your own Charles Schwab account, knowing about the market and the role it plays (and *can* play) in your retirement can better prepare you for any stormy waters ahead.

Where the Market Matters

On a submarine, you don't have to see the ocean to feel its pull. You learn to read the gauges, trust the instruments, and understand what the water is doing around you. Retirement is similar. Once you know how to read the "gauges" on the tools you already have, you can make sense of what's happening beneath the surface.

Let's look at some of the ways the market influences your retirement—whether you see it or not.

Pensions

Pensions feel insulated from the market because your monthly check never changes. Whether the S&P has a banner year or the Dow drops a thousand points, your benefit shows up the same. But beneath that steady surface, pension funds are some of the largest investors in the market. They buy stocks, bonds, real estate, and all kinds of market-linked assets because they have to produce long-term growth to meet their obligations.

You don't feel the swings because your employer or your state absorbs the volatility for you, but that doesn't mean the waves aren't moving. The market is the force that allows those checks to keep coming.

Employer Retirement Plans

Employer plans, such as 401(k)s, 403(b)s, and the Thrift Savings Plan, are usually where the market becomes more visible. If it's a good market year, your balance climbs. If it's a rough one, your statement reflects it. That isn't a design flaw—it's how these plans grow over time.

Most plans use a handful of common investment types. Target-date funds are the default for many people; they start heavier in stocks when you're younger and gradually shift toward more conservative holdings as you approach retirement. Broad market index funds track well-known market benchmarks, giving you exposure to large numbers of companies at once without a manager trying to outsmart the market. Stock funds are often split by company size: Large-cap funds focus on established giants with long track records, while small-cap funds invest in younger, smaller companies with more room for growth but more volatility. And bond funds invest in debt rather than stock, offering steadier movement but still responding to interest-rate changes.

Once people learn how to read their plan statements—recognizing names like S&P 500 Index Fund, Large-Cap Blend, or Target Retirement 2035—they suddenly realize they've been market participants all along. They just didn't know the vocabulary.

Income-Producing Insurance Products

We talked a bit in chapter 6 about annuities and other insurance tools that can create dependable retirement income. We'll dive deeper into those in the next chapter, but let's talk just a little here about their connection to the market.

With these products, your money isn't directly invested in stocks or bonds the way it is in a 401(k). But the interest or crediting you earn is tied to a market index. When the index rises, the insurance company may credit interest based on that performance. When the index falls, you don't lose money—you simply don't earn interest for that period.

It's like standing safely inside a submarine while monitoring sonar. You're not physically out in the waves, but the behavior of the water still informs what you see on your screen. These products use the market as a measuring tool while insulating your principal from market losses.

Indexes That Drive Retirement Accounts

Let's dive a little deeper into these indexes we keep talking about. A lot of market anxiety comes from not knowing what the market actually is or that most of the heavy lifting inside retirement plans is tied to just a few key indexes.

The most familiar, of course, is the S&P 500. This is a list of five hundred of the largest, most well-known companies in America. I often tell people the S&P is like the "varsity team" of the market. They're big names, household brands, companies whose logos you probably see five times before lunch. What many folks don't realize is that all S&P stocks aren't created equal; this index is weighted, meaning the biggest companies—tech giants like Apple, Microsoft, and Amazon—carry a lot more influence than the smaller ones. So when tech has a strong year, the S&P tends to look great. When it stumbles, the index feels it. Understanding that basic idea helps people make sense of why their 401(k) might swing more in some years and less in others, even when their contributions stay the same.

Then there's the Dow Jones Industrial Average, or just "the Dow." It's older, smaller, and a little more "old school." Instead of tracking five hundred companies, it tracks just thirty of the blue-chip giants that have been around for decades. These are companies that make the things we use every day or provide services we don't think twice about because they've always been there. The Dow doesn't move as dramatically as the S&P because it's full of steady performers. It's the index people look at when they want to know whether the overall mood of the market is optimistic or nervous. If the S&P is the varsity team, the Dow is the veterans holding the line.

And then we have the Russell 2000, which tracks small and midsized companies—businesses that aren't household names yet but make up the backbone of the American economy. These companies don't get as much press as the tech titans, but they give a truer sense of what's happening across the broader market. When the Russell is struggling, it often means smaller businesses are feeling pressure. When the Russell is thriving, it usually signals a healthier, more confident economy at large. A lot of employer plans include funds tied to this index because it helps balance out the influence of those big S&P players.

There are other indexes, but these three set the tone for most retirement accounts. They're yardsticks. They tell fund managers—and, indirectly, you—how the market's different moving parts are behaving. When you own a target-date fund or a broad market fund, what you really own is a bundle of these indexes stitched together. Your retirement plan isn't betting on hundreds of individual companies. It's just following the scoreboards that track them.

Once you understand how these indexes work, you don't need to analyze charts or memorize ticker symbols to make sense of your retirement. You just need to know which indexes your plan leans on and what each of them generally represents. That simple knowledge turns a frightening mystery into something manageable, predictable, and surprisingly logical.

If the S&P has a big day, your account probably had a decent one too. If the Dow is sluggish, your steadier holdings might be as well. If the Russell is surging, your small-cap exposure is probably smiling. It's not day-to-day prediction—it's awareness. And awareness is half the battle when it comes to feeling less shaken by the headlines.

Bringing It All Together

Understanding the market's role in your retirement isn't about becoming an expert or learning how to pick stocks. It's about recognizing that the market is already woven into almost every tool you're counting on.

Once people understand that, the whole picture changes. Those statements they get in the mail start making more sense. The headlines feel a little less scary. And the normal ups and downs of the market stop feeling like personal threats because they finally understand what's happening under the surface. It's amazing how much calmer things feel once the mystery is gone.

The market isn't something to run from. It's simply part of the environment you're navigating. And when you know what's driving your benefits and balances, you're in a far better position to stay level and keep your retirement on course.

CHAPTER 8

INSURANCE THAT WORKS

When people hear the word *insurance*, most of them think about their homeowner's policy, their auto coverage, or their health plan. That kind of insurance, while it certainly has its place and provides important peace of mind, is more like the outer hull of a submarine—important, necessary, and built to protect you from obvious dangers, but not something that powers the vessel or keeps the mission moving.

The insurance we'll be discussing in this chapter works much deeper in your financial system. It's more like the internal compartments that manage pressure, stabilize the environment, and keep everything functioning the way it should when conditions change. Some of these tools protect your money from risks the market can't control. Others help support or even produce income in retirement. And a few of them can solve problems before they ever hit your radar.

My goal when you're my client isn't to turn you into an insurance expert or hand you a stack of products to study. It's to show you how the right kinds of insurance fit into your retirement plan and why they matter. Unlike many financial professionals, I'm not tied to any single carrier, so if I don't like what one company is doing, I can go to another without missing a beat. I also make sure every company we work with follows disclosure requirements, including commission transparency. I don't have to do this, and compensation will *never* drive my recommendations. I just feel it's my fiduciary duty to choose insurance products based only on long-term favorability and value—period. All that matters to me (which is also what matters the most to my clients) is putting you in a position where your plan stays steady no matter what's happening above the surface.

Life Insurance That Does More Than Pay a Benefit

Many of the folks I talk to don't know that life insurance can be a lot more than a check someone gets after they're gone. That's certainly part of it—and for families with kids at home or big financial obligations, that death benefit matters a lot. But in retirement planning, the life insurance tools I use are built for more than protection. They can grow money without market downside, give you flexible access to cash when you need it, and in some cases even help support your income.

One of the most useful of these types of life insurance is indexed universal life (IUL).

One of its biggest advantages is how it handles market movement. The interest that gets credited to your policy is tied to an index. If the index goes up, your policy can earn interest up to whatever cap the carrier sets. If the index drops, you don't lose a penny. You just earn zero for that period. That safety floor can play a big role in retirement planning—steady beats scary every time.

But where these policies really shine is later in life, when you need flexibility. You can use the cash value to supplement income, pay for a major purchase, help a child or grandchild, or get through a season when you need extra breathing room. Some families even use these policies to help with college costs—we'll talk more about that in a later chapter. With IUL policies, money grows safely and can be accessed when life calls for it.

Another benefit of IUL? Loans from these policies come from the general fund of the insurance company, not from your own account. That means your policy keeps performing even while you borrow against it, so you're not hitting the pause button on your growth. And in some states (like Ohio), your IUL policy's cash value is also protected from creditors—one of those quiet advantages people don't always think about until they wish they had.

Life insurance isn't just about what happens when you're gone. When it's structured right, it becomes a flexible tool that strengthens your income plan, your tax plan, and your long-term protection. But life insurance is only one part of that picture. Another piece—one most people don't think about until life forces the issue—is long-term care.

Preparing for Long-Term Care

Nobody pictures themselves needing help with daily activities or spending months or years in a nursing care facility. I get it. I don't love thinking about it either. But about one in three people will face a long-term care (LTC) event at some point in their life. Ignoring that fact doesn't make it go away. It just makes everything worse when it happens.

What most people don't realize is how expensive LTC really is. A nursing home stay can run seven to nine thousand dollars a month in many areas—more in some parts of the country. And in-home care isn't far behind. If you bring in an aide for even a few hours a day, the costs pile up quickly. Add nights or weekends, and you're staring at bills that can drain a lifetime of savings before you know it.

The hardest part for many families is discovering that almost none of this is covered by traditional health insurance. Medicare helps with short-term rehab after a hospital stay, but once you stabilize, the coverage stops. It doesn't pay for someone to help you bathe, dress, prepare meals, or stay safe in your own home. Those services are considered custodial care—exactly the kind of care most people end up needing—and they're paid for out of pocket unless you have a plan in place.

I've seen families try to manage those costs on their own, and it's heartbreaking. Retirement plans that looked solid suddenly crack and spring leaks under the pressure. Adult children feel torn between caring for a parent and caring for their own families. Savings disappear. Stress skyrockets. It's not the kind of burden anyone wants to leave to the people they love. That's why planning for long-term care matters—because the financial and emotional weight of going without a plan is far heavier than most people expect.

LTC insurance is, for most folks, out of reach. These policies are priced like health insurance, which means the companies can raise premiums whenever their costs go up. And boy, have they gone up. I've seen families hit with rate increases of 30, 40, even 50 percent. Some people eventually had to drop their coverage, not because they didn't want it anymore but because they couldn't afford to keep it.

That's a good way to sink a retirement ship.

Instead of LTC insurance, I recommend life insurance policies with long-term care riders. These riders let you convert your death benefit into a monthly income stream if you need long-term care. It's simple: If you don't need care, your family receives the full death benefit, and if you do, you get the money while you're alive, paid out over time. There are no surprise premium increases because the policy is underwritten based on mortality instead of unpredictable healthcare costs. Once it's issued, the premium can't be raised.

This approach solves several problems at once. You're protected without having to worry about rising premiums. You keep control of your plan. And you avoid the slow financial bleed that can happen when long-term care expenses start stacking up.

Annuities: Income You Can Count On

As I mentioned earlier in the book, annuities tend to stir up strong opinions, and most of that comes from misunderstandings. We already covered the nuts and bolts back in chapter 6, so I won't repeat any of that here. Instead, let me show you how annuities fit into the bigger system of retirement income—because that's where they really earn their keep.

When I'm looking at a client's income plan, one of the first questions I ask myself is simple: *Where is the guaranteed income going to come from?* Social Security helps, but for many families it's not enough to cover the basics, let alone handle inflation or unexpected expenses. Investments can fill part of the gap, but markets don't always behave. You don't want your monthly income tied to whether the market wakes up in a good mood.

That's where annuities can play a role. They're one of the few tools that can turn a portion of your savings into steady, predictable income—a paycheck you can count on no matter what the market does. In submarine terms, it's like having a dedicated power source that doesn't flicker when the rest of the system gets stressed. You still need the rest of the vessel running, but that stable power keeps everything from rattling apart during choppy conditions.

Different annuities serve different purposes. For some families, an annuity acts as the "income floor"—a guarantee that their basic living expenses will always be covered. For others, it becomes a way to delay drawing from their investments, giving their portfolio more time to recover after a downturn. And for some, it's about peace of mind. I've seen people relax visibly once they know a portion of their income is locked in for life.

Another reason annuities come up in planning is because they don't lose value when the market drops. From a planning standpoint, that stability can protect you from one of the biggest threats in retirement: having to pull income from your investments while the market is falling. A good annuity structure can take that pressure off your portfolio so you're not forced into bad timing.

Now, do I use annuities for everyone? No. They're tools, not magic wands. But for the families they fit, they can bring structure, stability, and predictability to a part of retirement that often feels uncertain. And when you combine that guaranteed income with the rest of your system—your Social Security, your investment strategy, your tax plan—you suddenly have a plan that can hold steady even when the market misbehaves.

The bottom line is simple: If you're trying to build a retirement income that lasts as long as you do, annuities deserve a place in the conversation. Not because they're perfect, and not because they're right for everyone but because they can solve problems that no other tool solves in quite the same way.

Bringing It All Together

Insurance doesn't show up at the top of most people's planning lists, but it should never be treated as an afterthought. In the submarine world, the systems that made the least noise were the ones that kept us alive when something unexpected happened. Insurance works the same way. It protects your money from losses you can't control. It keeps pressure from building when life throws a curve. And in many cases, it becomes part of the income structure that keeps your retirement steady.

Investments help your money grow. Insurance helps your money endure. Both matter. Both play a role. When you see them working together through the Retirement Periscope, you start to understand how a real plan stays stable in both calm seas and choppy ones.

A good retirement plan isn't built on luck. It's built on understanding the system, preparing for what you can't see coming, and using the right tools in the right way. Insurance—used wisely—is one of those tools that keeps the whole vessel afloat.

CHAPTER 9

TAXES DON'T RETIRE

Whether you like it or not, if you're an American, taxes are part of your life. There's a good reason that old "death and taxes" quote by Ben Franklin is still around. And he made that quote long before we even had *income* tax. In fact, the US Tax Code back then wasn't even called that—it was basically just a few pages of a tariff act. Today it's thousands of pages and millions of words, constantly expanding and reshaping our financial playing field.

It can seem like every dollar we make and every we dollar we spend—both before and after retirement—are subject to some sort of taxation. That's probably because, at least to a certain extent, they are.

But not always.

It's my job to scope out where this applies to your financial plans, where every "not always" can matter most. In this chapter, I'll take a bit of a deeper dive into taxes—and how they can affect your retirement more than you realize.

Taxes in Retirement

If a submarine springs a leak, it isn't automatically a death sentence for the crew. Submarines are built with watertight compartments that can be sealed off in an emergency, keeping the rest of the vessel stable, safe, and dry. Your retirement can't be so easily compartmentalized; one tax torpedo can sink the whole ship.

And, unless you know where to look, you won't even see it coming.

Folks who try to DIY their retirement often view taxes as a completely separate entity. Ask them about tax planning, and they answer, "Well, I *plan* to let my CPA handle it" or "I *plan* to file online, just like always." But that's not planning, is it? That's reacting. It's compliance instead of strategy. It's history.

If you'll allow me a non-nautical metaphor, that's like looking in the rearview mirror instead of through the windshield at the road ahead. That doesn't work for financial planning in general. It *really* doesn't work for retirement planning.

I'm old enough to remember when smoking was allowed on airplanes. They usually delegated the smoking section to a few rows in the back, but there often wasn't any sort of divider between the two sections. I always found that somewhat comical. Last time I checked, smoke can't read. It's going to go wherever the air goes.

Social Security

Same goes for taxes, which also stink. For instance, taxes can stink up your Social Security by drifting right into it at the worst possible time. A lot of folks believe Social Security is tax-free because they already paid taxes on that money once. Makes sense in theory, but that's not how the IRS looks at it. They use something called "provisional income"—basically half your Social Security plus most of your other income—to decide whether your benefit gets taxed. Cross the wrong line at the wrong time, and suddenly up to 85 percent of your Social Security becomes taxable.

Here's where things get interesting. Most people don't realize that withdrawals from their individual retirement account (IRA) and 401(k) count toward that provisional income. So the moment you take a big distribution to buy a car, fix the roof, or help a grandchild with college, you might unknowingly trigger taxes on your Social Security. That's when people come into my office saying, "I don't understand why my refund disappeared." Well, smoke drifts.

I once worked with a gentleman who loved giving to charity. Every year, he would bring me an inch-and-a-half-thick folder full of receipts he felt obligated to itemize. When he hit the age when he had to start pulling required minimum distributions (RMDs), he said, "I don't need the money, and I sure don't want the tax bill." So we switched him to qualified charitable distributions—sending his RMDs straight to the charities he supported. That move alone knocked about $40,000 off his taxable income for the year, and because that income never technically hit his return, it also lowered the amount of his Social Security that got taxed. Better outcome, more generous results, and no more paper mountain.

Investments

Taxes don't just drift into Social Security, though. They sneak into your investments too. A lot of people focus on what they're invested in, not how those investments are taxed. But the "wrapper"—traditional IRA, Roth IRA, brokerage account—is just as important as the investment itself. Put the wrong asset in the wrong place, and you're volunteering for taxes you didn't need to pay.

I've seen clients keep their highest-growth investments inside traditional IRAs, which means every bit of that growth gets taxed as ordinary income later. Meanwhile, the Roth—whose growth comes out tax-free—was full of investments that were barely moving. Same money, different placement, huge difference in taxes down the line.

And timing matters. One client wanted to cash out a large chunk of his IRA to buy land and build a house. If he had yanked the whole thing at once, the tax bill would've been . . . well, "horrific" might be too light a word. Instead, we structured his withdrawals to line up with each construction phase. He took what he needed when he needed it and let the rest stay invested and grow. Over two or three tax years, that approach saved him over $30,000 in taxes. Same land, same house, completely different financial outcome.

Insurance

Then there's the way taxes weave through your insurance decisions. Most people don't think of life insurance as having anything to do with taxes until a mistake proves otherwise. I've seen people list their estate as the beneficiary, thinking they were being organized. What actually happens is the death benefit gets dragged into the estate and can become taxable when it didn't have to be. Or someone forgets to change a beneficiary after a divorce and an ex-spouse ends up inheriting a retirement account or old policy worth hundreds of thousands of dollars because beneficiary designations override wills. That's not a tax problem on the surface, but it creates tax problems for the people left behind. Mistakes compound.

Even long-term care or hybrid policies can have tax consequences if they're not handled correctly. Some allow for tax-advantaged exchanges or tax-free benefits, but only if you structure them the right way. This is why I tell people insurance isn't separate from the rest of their plan. It's connected to everything—just like those compartments on a submarine that look isolated but share valves, wiring, and air systems. A pressure change in one affects the others.

Legacy Planning

And then there's legacy planning, which we'll talk more about in the next chapter. A lot of folks think legacy planning is just making sure they have a will. A will is important, but it doesn't stop the tax implications that can hit your heirs long after you're gone. The kids who inherit your traditional IRA, for example, now have to empty it within ten years. If they're in their peak earning years, that money gets piled on top of their income, and suddenly the inheritance you hoped would bless them ends up pushing them into higher tax brackets. A Roth IRA solves that problem, but only if you think about it before it becomes their problem.

I've also seen situations when someone passed away without any estate documents at all. In those cases, the government effectively decides who gets what. And believe me, the government's plan is never the most tax-efficient one. I've worked with families whose grief was compounded by tax surprises, probate delays, or assets tied up because no one had legal authority to move them. The emotional cost is just as real as the financial one.

All of this is why I don't treat taxes as a separate part of the plan. Taxes are the air system running beneath everything. Change the pressure in one compartment and you feel it everywhere else. Retirement works the same way—your Social Security, investments, insurance, and legacy plan are all connected. A smart move in one area can save you money in another. A careless move in one area can cost you money in all of them.

Bringing It All Together

When you get right down to it, taxes are less about numbers and more about consequences. Every decision you make in retirement affects something else, sometimes immediately and sometimes quietly in the background. Social Security, investments, insurance, the legacy you leave behind—none of these pieces stand alone. They're part of the same system, whether you realize it or not.

That's why tax planning isn't a once-a-year chore. It's an ongoing part of your financial life, woven into everything from how you take distributions to how you structure charity to how you protect your family. When you understand where the fumes can drift and how to control them, you end up keeping more of what you've earned. And you sleep better at night knowing the IRS isn't getting invited to dinner any more than necessary.

That's the whole goal: clarity, confidence, and a plan that works in the real world, not just on paper.

CHAPTER 10

LEAVING A LEGACY

Much of financial planning—and especially retirement planning—is devoted to ensuring we don't run out of money before we run out of life. We strategize to enjoy our golden years without becoming a burden to our kids or other family members. Some folks, including many I call clients and friends, really aspire to nothing more than that.

But, at some point, we *will* run out of life. And even if you aren't able to provide for your grandkids' education or endow your favorite charity, you'll still need a plan.

Someone once said that a legacy isn't what you leave *to* people, but what you leave *in* them. I find this a beautiful and profound sentiment—we all know the most important things in life aren't measured in dollars and cents. We're all looking to create a lifetime of memories and leave a legacy of meaning and purpose. Traits like integrity, kindness, and honesty can't be included in a will.

However, there's also a whole lot that *can* be included in a will. And there's lots of potential to make mistakes that can result in needless headaches and expenses for your loved ones, both during those stressful times after your passing and perhaps for years to come.

This is exactly what a good retirement plan is created to avoid.

In this chapter, we'll look at some things you'll need to know to ensure a lasting legacy—whether you're leaving behind wealth or just peace of mind.

A Legacy of Learning

We've all heard the cliché "Give a man a fish and feed him for a day; teach him to fish and feed him for a lifetime." It's a cliché because it's true. And here's another truth, same principle: One of the most valuable legacies you can leave your heirs isn't money itself; it's the knowledge and discipline to manage it.

I don't know why or how, but somewhere along the way, talking about money with our kids became taboo. Maybe it stems from hard times and the shame some of our parents and grandparents felt about finances that seemed perpetually underwater. Or maybe it's just always been like that.

Either way, it's a taboo that's fostered an epidemic of financial illiteracy, setting kids up for rough seas right out of port. It's a taboo begging for a torpedo.

I'm not saying you should teach your kids or grandkids to do your taxes (not yet anyway). But treating family finances as more of a family affair will serve them well when they have to pay their own way. Of course, I'm a money geek. I love talking with anyone about money—whether I'm speaking with teens in local 4-H and FFA programs about the importance of saving (I tell them, "Start now. Start small. Just start"), helping my granddaughter with her high school personal finance course, or walking a client and their adult children through the creation of a trust.

Finances aren't to be feared. They're to be faced and—with a little knowledge and some discipline—conquered. That's a legacy that doesn't cost anything but will pay dividends for a lifetime.

A Legacy of Peace of Mind

Whether relatively simple or incredibly complex, legacy plans are as unique as the legacies left behind. But what they all have in common is their core function: providing your heirs with clarity and peace of mind. Give them direction. Give them a clean path forward so they aren't forced to make decisions while they're grieving. You don't want your family guessing about what you wanted or fighting through a pile of paperwork to find answers. You want them to be able to breathe, focus on each other, and settle your affairs without running an obstacle course.

That starts with a will. I've seen, far too often, what happens when someone passes without one. In that situation, the state steps in with the laws of intestacy. And trust me on this: You probably won't like the state's plan. It's written by lawmakers who never met you and have no idea what your wishes were. Your assets get divided based on formulas—not family dynamics, not fairness, and certainly not common sense.

But even a will isn't enough on its own. Many people don't realize that beneficiary designations override everything else. You could have the most beautifully written will in the world, but if your old 401(k) still names an ex-spouse as the beneficiary, guess who gets the money? I once worked with a man whose ex-wife was still listed on a retirement account worth over a million dollars. If he had passed before updating it, it wouldn't have mattered what his intentions were for that money or what his will said. Needless to say, he was pretty relieved that I caught that. His ex-wife, probably not so much.

Another thing I warn people about is naming the estate as a beneficiary. On paper it sounds tidy, but in practice it can turn a tax-free payout into a taxable mess. It can also tie up money in probate for months—or years—when your family may need it right away. These are the kinds of mistakes that don't feel big in the moment, but as we've seen, even a small valve left half-open can flood a compartment.

And then there's the human side of all this. A good legacy plan isn't just documents—it's communication. It's that "family affair" I talked about earlier. I don't get clients' adult children involved because I'm trying to drum up business. I do it so that, when the time comes, those kids will know what to expect and where to go for help. They need a trusted guide who already understands the family layout, the accounts, and the intentions behind every decision. That simple step can prevent family conflict, delays, and the "Now what?" panic that often follows a loss.

Finally, don't forget the practical details: burial or cremation preferences, locations of important paperwork, the name of your executor, and billing or subscription accounts that need to be closed. These things aren't pleasant to talk about, but they're a tremendous gift. They spare your loved ones from stress at the exact moment when they're least able to handle it. Peace of mind isn't about money but about removing uncertainty. When your affairs are clearly laid out, your family can focus on honoring your memory instead of sorting out your paperwork.

A Legacy of Education

When it comes to financial and retirement planning, one of the first things folks dream about—beyond wanting to ensure that they're not a burden to their kids—is being able to pay for their children's education. That dream often pre-dates any thoughts of retirement and is a legacy that you'll hopefully be around to witness.

Education planning usually begins with good intentions and a lot of confusion. Most folks are familiar with the idea of a 529 plan, and there's nothing wrong with having one. In fact, I encourage parents to set up a small one for their teenager, not as the main strategy but as a teaching tool. Let the child put money into it from part-time jobs or birthday gifts. It gives them skin in the game and teaches them how savings grow.

But relying on a 529 plan alone can be risky. These plans are fully exposed to the market, and I often joke that during 2008, many 529s turned into 229s. (Believe it or not, that's funny to my industry friends.) Parents saving faithfully for years suddenly found their education funds cut nearly in half. I don't like leaving something that important up to chance.

That's why, for long-term planning, I often use life insurance with cash value—those indexed universal life policies we talked about earlier—as the backbone of college funding. They grow tax-deferred, participate in market gains, and avoid losses in market downturns. And unlike 529 plans, that money isn't locked into education. If your child doesn't go to college, the funds can be redirected—toward a first home, a wedding, or even supplementing your own retirement one day.

Another major advantage is how these strategies affect financial aid. Some assets count heavily against a student when colleges calculate aid eligibility. Others don't. Structuring things correctly can make a meaningful difference in award letters and out-of-pocket costs. Families are often shocked by how much ground they're giving up simply because no one explained how the system works.

Over the years, I've also helped many families navigate the confusing world of admissions, financial aid offers, and appeals. Most people don't know you can appeal a college's financial aid offer, but you can. And in many cases, it works. Colleges want successful alumni. They're often willing to reconsider when families make a thoughtful case. Knowing how to evaluate an offer, compare it to others from similar schools, and respond strategically can save tens of thousands of dollars and keep a young adult from starting life weighed down by debt.

A Legacy of Charity

I've always believed that giving is one of the purest reflections of what matters to us. It tells the story of a person's heart as clearly as anything we could put in writing. And for many of my clients, supporting their church, their food pantry, or a cause that shaped their lives is a legacy they want to continue long after they're gone.

For those already in retirement, there are ways to give that are both generous and efficient. One of the most powerful is directing money straight from a retirement account to a qualified charity. When done correctly, this can satisfy required withdrawals while keeping that money from ever becoming taxable income.

That single move can solve several problems at once. It allows you to give more without increasing your tax bill. It can help keep more of your Social Security benefits from being taxed. And it simplifies recordkeeping by removing the need to itemize or track stacks of donation receipts. It's one of the rare moments when generosity and efficiency line up perfectly.

For many families, this becomes part of an annual rhythm, a way to continue supporting the people and organizations they love without complicating their financial picture. A legacy of charity isn't measured by the size of the gift. It's measured by the intention behind it. Whether you're giving a little or a lot, the impact carries forward, echoing far beyond the dollars themselves.

Bringing It All Together

Legacy planning isn't just about money. It's about responsibility. It's about clarity. It's about making life easier for the people you care about most. You're not just planning for the end of life. You're strengthening your family today. You're giving them confidence, direction, and a foundation that can last for decades.

In this section of the book, we've talked about retirement income, investments, insurance, taxes, and legacy, not as isolated topics but as connected components of the same system. Every gauge matters. Every decision matters. Now that you know more about that system, it's time to look through the Retirement Periscope and see how a new outlook can help ensure smooth sailing.

THE PROCESS THAT BRINGS IT ALL TOGETHER

The Retirement Periscope™ in Action

CHAPTER 11

DISCOVER A NEW OUTLOOK

A lot of naval submarine training takes place in a regular ole classroom. Recruits don't get to hop right on the sub. First they get taught everything they need to know to get it right once they dive in. If you were lucky enough to have driver's ed taught at your high school, you get the idea: There's a lot to learn before they let you behind the wheel.

So far, our journey into financial and retirement planning has been a similar classroom phase. We've been building understanding—learning the language, the instruments, and the logic behind the decisions most people are asked to make without ever being properly trained. You've seen why certain questions matter, why shortcuts can be dangerous, and why well-intentioned advice often falls short when it isn't part of a bigger plan.

That kind of groundwork isn't glamorous, but it's essential. On a submarine, nobody wants to discover in the middle of a dive that they misunderstood how a system works. The learning has to happen first, in a controlled environment, where mistakes are cheap and corrections are easy. The same is true with money. It's far better to understand how decisions behave before you have to rely on them to carry you through this phase of life.

In this closing section of the book, we'll let you test-drive a partnership with our Outlook Financial Center team to plan a safe and secure trip into the future. I'll walk you through each of the four distinct stages of our journey together—discovery, design, deployment, and monitoring/course correction—providing you with details of what to expect and how to best be prepared. And don't worry; the principles I share with you in the following chapters can help you plan your financial path forward whether you become an Outlook client or not. Other financial planners and *most* financial advisors may take a bit of a different approach to their specific strategies and processes, but the underlying financial principles don't change.

It All Begins with Discovery

Your "retirement discovery" with our team isn't just a matter of finding out more about you and your financial goals and challenges; it's also your opportunity to find out more about us. This process often starts long before you ever pick up the phone. Maybe you saw me or Lori talking about finances on TV, then checked out our website and read some of our blogs. Maybe you even read a certain book . . .

Regardless of the exact route you took to get here, you've started at least *thinking* about your retirement—and now you're taking steps to find out more. Those first steps of discovery are huge! But we're still just skimming the surface.

For me and my team, discovery usually begins with a phone call or Zoom meeting. That first conversation isn't about selling anything. It's about figuring out whether we're a good fit for one another. I'll usually ask a few simple questions to get a sense of what prompted the call and what concerns are top of mind. More importantly, I'm listening for three things:

1. Are you looking for real solutions?

2. Are you willing to do the work that planning requires?

3. Are you prepared to be honest with us?

If the answer to any of those is no, that's okay—but it means we're probably not the right crew for this voyage.

Data Gathering

If we decide to work together, then we move forward with what I call our data-gathering meeting. This is when discovery gets serious.

Here's the part some people find uncomfortable, so I like to be up-front about it: We can't give professional answers without complete and accurate information. I don't ask for documents because I'm nosy. I just don't have time to be nosy. I ask because missing information is how people hit unseen obstacles.

On a submarine, you don't dive without knowing the fuel level, the depth rating, and the condition of every major system. Financial planning works the same way. And just like in a naval mission, sensitive information is closely guarded—we use a secure file storage platform for client communication, disclosures, and tax documents.

Before or shortly after that first meeting, we'll ask you to gather some core information so we can see the whole picture. That typically includes both core financial documents and debt and liability information. Here's what you'll need to compile:

Core financial documents

- Recent tax returns

- Income records, such as W-2s or earnings statements

- Statements for bank accounts, investment accounts, and retirement plans

- Pension or Social Security information, if applicable

- Life, health, and long-term care insurance policies

- Current wills or trust documents

Debt and liability information

- List of monthly expenses

- Mortgage statements

- Credit card, student loan, auto loan, or other outstanding debt statements

We'll also need details about your family health history even though I typically begin with a baseline planning horizon of ninety years old for my clients. That age isn't arbitrary. Statistically, if a married couple reaches age sixty-five, there's a nearly 50 percent chance that at least one spouse will live to age ninety. Planning for anything less creates a real risk of running out of money simply because you lived longer than expected. Family history helps us fine-tune that horizon and often extend it even further, but we always aim to err on the conservative side.

I had a client tell me that no men in his family had ever lived past age seventy. Did we factor that into his plan? Absolutely! We were able to help him retire at sixty-two so that if he adhered to the family tradition, he would have more time with his family and friends. But did we also plan out to age ninety so that he wouldn't go broke if he bucked the odds? You bet! We would much rather plan for extra years we don't need than need extra years we didn't plan for.

I know all that seems like a lot of information to gather—and it is—but every piece matters. Leaving something out is like covering a gauge and hoping for the best. We don't guess. We verify.

That first data meeting is also a conversation. We'll talk about your concerns, your family, and what prompted you to reach out in the first place. Sometimes we'll identify missing pieces and send you home with a little homework. That's normal. Discovery isn't rushed, because getting it right here makes everything else safer and smoother later.

To that end, we also record every meeting, whether we're speaking in person, on the phone, or online. We use state-of-the-art AI notetaking software designed to automatically redact sensitive information (Social Security numbers, account numbers, birthdays, etc.) while also ensuring no critical piece of information slips through any cracks. Just like in a submarine, cracks in any financial or retirement plan can be devastating.

Goals on the Horizon

Once we understand where you are, the next step is talking about where you want to go.

This part of discovery focuses on your goals—not in a technical sense yet, but in real-life terms. We're not designing a plan at this stage. We're listening and clarifying. Think of it as setting your destination before we ever plot a course.

Some goals are practical. Others are personal. Most are a mix of both. These are some common examples:

- Targeting a certain date/age to retire or slow down

- Living a specific retirement lifestyle day-to-day

- Traveling

- Helping children, grandchildren, or other family members

- Buying land, a boat, or a second home

- Giving to church or charities

- Making sure a spouse is protected

There are no right or wrong answers here, and you're allowed to pick as many as you like. My job (or any good financial planner's job) during this phase isn't to judge the feasibility of your goals—it's to understand them.

We'll also touch on risk tolerance. This is simply a way of understanding how much market movement you're comfortable with before it starts keeping you up at night. Some people can shrug off ups and downs. Others feel stress quickly. Neither is wrong, but it matters.

This is also where conversation matters more than charts. I don't believe in burying people under spreadsheets or financial jargon during these early meetings. Instead we talk things through using plain language and real-life examples. I often use stories—scenarios people can picture—to explain how markets behave and what different choices can feel like in the real world. It's the same approach I'm using in this book. If you understand the idea behind them, the numbers make a lot more sense later.

And yes, I've been known to get a little long-winded if a story runs away from me. That's where Lori comes in. If I start circling the periscope one too many times, she'll give me a well-timed nudge under the table to rein it back in. The goal isn't to impress you—it's to make sure you leave understanding what matters without feeling overwhelmed.

At this stage, we're not choosing investments or strategies. That begins in our next phase (and in the next chapter). For now, we're just identifying your comfort level so that our future recommendations make sense. Risk tolerance is part of goal-setting because a plan that looks good on paper but causes constant anxiety isn't a good plan at all.

Discovery is about clarity. It's about making sure we understand your destination, your concerns, and the kind of journey you want before we ever start drawing lines on the chart.

Bringing It All Together

Discovery is the foundation of everything that follows. It's when we slow down, gather the facts, and make sure we're all looking at the same set of instruments. Without it, planning becomes guesswork. With it, planning becomes intentional.

In this chapter, you've seen how the process begins: an initial conversation, careful data gathering, and honest discussions about goals and comfort levels. Nothing fancy. Nothing rushed. Just good preparation.

In the next chapter, we'll take everything we uncovered during discovery and move into design. This is when the real engineering begins. It's when we start connecting the dots, evaluating options, and building a plan that fits your life, your goals, and your tolerance for risk.

You wouldn't dive without a plan, and you shouldn't retire without one either.

CHAPTER 12

DESIGN YOUR TOMORROW

Financial and retirement plans—just like submarine missions—are all about using assets, strategies, and tactics to accomplish realistic goals. And just as assets on a sub mission aren't limited to the ship and its weapons system, the assets of your financial future include more than just your money and property. Your assets are your *tools*. During the discovery phase, we inventoried those assets and had a long conversation to get a better sense of your situation and your broader goals and objectives.

In this chapter, we turn our Retirement Periscope on the design phase to further define and refine those goals and objectives as we create strategies that best utilize the available tools.

That's just a fancy way of saying, "Now that we know what we're working with and have a good idea of where we want to go, let's find the best way to get there."

Findings Meeting

Usually seven to ten working days after we conclude our discovery phase, we'll get together (as always, in person or via Zoom) to discuss in greater depth the "what we're working with" and "where we want to go" parts of the equation. This is when Lori and I give you the good, the bad, and the ugly about how well those two elements are playing together.

It usually isn't quite what you were expecting. But here's the thing—clarity beats comfort every time. You can choose to look through your periscope, but that doesn't mean you won't find an enemy ship floating above you.

Sometimes a couple comes in convinced they'll both be able to retire at age sixty-two. They've done a lot right: contributed steadily to a 401(k), stayed out of major debt, maybe even paid off the house. On the surface, it feels like the end of the mission is in sight. Then we start stress-testing that goal—taxes, inflation, healthcare costs, Social Security timing, how income actually flows in retirement—and the math tells a harder truth. Retiring early can mean locking in lower Social Security for life, paying hefty health insurance premiums for several years, and pulling from investments faster than they can reasonably support. In cases like that, you might see leaks are likely in some compartments.

Other times, the issue isn't timing but expectations. A couple may want to maintain a lifestyle that simply isn't supported by their guaranteed income sources. That doesn't mean retirement is off the table. It means we have to redesign the mission: maybe work a little longer, adjust spending, or rethink what "retirement" really means. Fewer knobs turned all at once. More control. Less risk.

And here's the part that often surprises people—even in those tougher moments, there are almost always creative solutions. Rarely is the answer "You're done. No options." More often it's "Okay, let's reroute." Maybe that means phasing into retirement, using part-time income strategically, adjusting tax timing, or rethinking when and how certain assets are used. This is engineering, not judgment. We're solving a problem, not delivering a verdict.

During this meeting, we'll also present a nominal, baseline plan, a first-pass design that gets something real down on paper. Based on everything we've learned, we outline a strategy that makes sense for *you*: Here's where you are, here's where you've told us you want to go, and here's a reasonable way to connect the two. This isn't carved in marble. You don't have to do it this way. But until you put a stake in the ground, you don't really have anything to react to.

At this stage, we're staying at the strategic level. We're talking about *approaches*, not specific companies or products.

No brand names. No implementation yet. The question here is simple: Do you like the direction? If the answer is yes, we can dig deeper and eventually deploy the tactics. If not, we adjust. That's the point.

Sometimes you'll be pleasantly surprised. Every now and then, someone sits down across from us bracing for bad news, fully planning to work until age sixty-five or longer because that's what they've always heard was "responsible." Then we map everything out and realize they're in far better shape than they thought. Maybe they've built more flexible after-tax savings than they realized. Maybe a pension, rental income, or modest lifestyle means their portfolio doesn't have to work nearly as hard. Sometimes the answer is "You know what? You could probably do this at sixty-two, and do it comfortably."

To me, the findings meeting is like charting a course on a nautical map; before the engines are started, the crew must first agree on the destination and the general path around the financial mines and obstacles. That's what the meeting is really about—aligning reality with intention. Sometimes that means recalibrating a dream so it's achievable. Other times it means telling folks that their Golden Years might be more golden and start sooner than they ever dreamed.

Welcome Aboard!

It's important to understand that no one becomes an official client until after the findings meeting. This means no dotted lines are signed and there's no commitment, no money changing hands. Up to now, it's about learning, gaining clarity, and deciding whether it even makes sense to move forward together. Only after the findings meeting—once you've seen the realities, understood the nominal plan, and had time to react to it—do we officially welcome you aboard.

That's when the real work begins.

Up to this point, we've been talking about direction. Now we start building structure around it. Not by jumping straight into products or companies—that comes later—but by making sure everything you already have is properly aligned and actually working together.

The first order of business is making sure all the financial documents we gathered during discovery are now fully organized, reviewed, and in good order, especially those beneficiary designations I warned you about. I know they're easy to overlook, but they matter more than most people realize. A beneficiary that's outdated or misaligned can undo years of careful planning, no matter how good the strategy looks on paper.

This step isn't about changing things yet. It's about visibility. You can't command a vessel if you don't know what's in each compartment or how it's currently configured.

Once that foundation is solid, we start putting real definition around the nominal plan. Think of that plan as the first sketch on a chart table. It gave us a general route. Now we start refining it—pressure-testing assumptions, tightening timelines, and making sure every major goal has a clear role in the overall mission.

That refinement doesn't happen all at once. Instead we break the work into focused, single-topic meetings. One meeting might deal only with investments. Another might focus solely on insurance, and another on taxes or income. The goal is simple: Get each area under control before moving on to the next.

Remember—this is still strategy, not implementation. We're talking about *how* your money should work and what available options can best make sure it gets the job done. We're deciding what needs to happen, in what order, and why. If something doesn't sit right, we adjust. If a goal needs to be reshaped, we do it here—before anything is locked in.

That's how we avoid unnecessary course corrections later.

Once they see the structure coming together, most people ask the same question, even if they don't phrase it this way: "How do we organize all this so it actually works when life gets messy?" That's where buckets come in.

A Different Kind of Bucket List

When most people hear the phrase *bucket list*, they think of things they would like to do before they die. Travel somewhere exotic. Buy something indulgent. Check off a few experiences they've been carrying around in their head for years. Most of the time, those lists are more aspirational than practical. They're nice ideas but not necessarily things they've planned for.

In financial and retirement planning, buckets aren't about unreachable dreams. They're about turning realistic goals into a system that actually works. Buckets give structure to your money. They break what usually feels like one big, overwhelming pile of accounts into purposeful, understandable pieces.

Most folks come in with what I call a "big glob." It might include a 401(k) from work, an IRA somewhere else, a savings account that's doing double or triple duty. Everything technically exists, but nothing is clearly assigned. And when money doesn't have a job, people either worry about all of it or ignore all of it. Neither works very well.

Buckets solve that problem by forcing us to answer one simple question for every dollar: What is this money supposed to do?

Once money has a purpose, everything else starts to make more sense: time horizon, risk level, amount of volatility you can tolerate, even how taxes should be handled. Instead of wondering how "the portfolio" is doing, you can look at each bucket and ask whether it's doing the job it was designed to do. That's a much calmer, more systematic and useful way to measure progress.

The mistake most people make—one the financial industry often encourages—is treating all money the same. But not all money lives on the same timeline, and it shouldn't be invested or managed the same way. Money you won't touch for twenty years can afford to ride out market ups and downs. Money you'll need in five years can't. Pretending otherwise doesn't make you disciplined. It makes you vulnerable.

Buckets let us respect those differences.

Some buckets are long-term by design. They're meant to support income far down the road, and they can tolerate volatility because time is on their side. Other buckets exist for goals that are closer or fixed in time, things like education expenses or major purchases. Those buckets need more stability because the penalty for bad timing is real. You don't get to tell a tuition bill to wait for the market to recover.

There are also buckets designed for flexibility—money that gives you options. These are often overlooked, but they matter more than people realize. Life doesn't follow a straight line, and having money that isn't locked into a single outcome can make a huge difference when circumstances change.

Another layer most people miss is how taxes fit in. Where taxable, tax-deferred, or tax-free money lives often matters more than what it's invested in. Two buckets can hold similar assets and behave very differently simply because of how they're taxed when you use them. That's why I spend so much time talking about structure instead of products. The wrapper around the money defines how flexible it really is.

This is also where bucketing separates real planning from asset gathering. Asset gatherers want everything in one place because it's easier for them to manage. I want things organized in a way that serves *you*. Buckets aren't designed to make statements look pretty but to make decisions easier and outcomes more predictable.

And there's another benefit people don't expect: Buckets reduce anxiety.

When the market drops—and it will—people with one big glob feel like *everything* is under attack. But people with buckets can look at the situation and say, "Okay, this bucket is exposed, but that one isn't. And this one doesn't matter for another ten years anyway." That perspective alone keeps people from making expensive emotional decisions at exactly the wrong time.

In submarine terms, it's the difference between knowing which compartment took on water and thinking the whole boat is sinking. Panic comes from not knowing. Structure brings calm.

Buckets don't eliminate risk. They organize it. They don't guarantee outcomes. They improve odds and turn vague ideas about the future into something you can actually manage.

That's the real point of this approach. It's not about complexity or cleverness. It's about building a system in which every piece of your money has a role, a reason, and a place so the life you want isn't left to chance. That's what a real bucket list looks like.

Bringing It All Together

A big part of planning your financial future is slowing down long enough to look honestly at where you are, deciding where you want to go, and then building a structure that gives you the best chance of getting there without unnecessary risk or stress.

The design phase is when intention meets reality. It's when assumptions get tested, trade-offs become clear, and vague ideas start taking shape as something workable. The findings meeting, the nominal plan, the process of getting organized, and the use of buckets are all part of the same objective: creating a system that ensures your money works with you instead of against you.

While much of what you've read in this chapter reflects how Lori and I approach planning, the underlying principles—as I've mentioned—apply far beyond our office. Any good financial professional (planner or advisor) should help you clarify goals, stress-test assumptions, organize resources by purpose, and think strategically before anything is implemented. If you understand what should be happening, you'll be better prepared no matter who you're working with.

Designing your tomorrow isn't a one-time effort. It's a disciplined way of thinking, one that brings clarity, flexibility, and confidence as life changes. Once the design is sound, the next step, deciding how to put it into motion, becomes much more straightforward. That's when we turn from design to deployment and begin translating strategy into action.

CHAPTER 13

DEPLOYMENT TIME

We Love It When a Plan Comes Together

If you really think about it, you've spent most of your life preparing for this mission. Our survival instinct is something we have in common with all God's creatures; preparing for our survival years (and even decades) in advance is one of the things that separates us from the rest.

And make no mistake: ensuring you won't run out of money before you run out of life *is* survival. Stress kills. Peace of mind, not so much.

You may not have actively thought about surviving retirement until recently, but that doesn't mean you haven't been preparing for it. You held a job. You took at least reasonable care of your health. If you're like many, the first time surviving retirement crossed your mind was when you filled out the paperwork for your first 401(k).

So, yes, the preparation for this moment has been going on for a while. As we wrap up our discover–design–deploy trilogy, we're going to take a look through the Retirement Periscope at this last—and ongoing—phase of what we all hope will be a long, rewarding, and well-managed journey.

Deployment: The Ultimate Preparation

When it comes right down to it, the best retirement planning can be summed up with two words: Be prepared. I think that would be an awesome motto for our industry if the Boy Scouts hadn't already taken it.

On a submarine mission, deployment doesn't mean we fire our torpedoes. It just means we move to a place in the ocean where—if we do have to engage—it'll do the most good.

That's what we do every day. And, as in many military missions, the greatest success is having to do nothing except be prepared.

What does this all look like through the Retirement Periscope? Well, it depends on your situation. Let's say you're a married couple in your early fifties, both working professionals, earning a combined household income of about $143,000 a year. You've been responsible. You've saved steadily in your workplace retirement plans, built a modest emergency fund, and kept your mortgage balance manageable. Nothing feels urgent, but nothing feels fully settled either.

Through the Retirement Periscope, we began by understanding how the pieces actually work together. One spouse may be counting on a pension, but that pension may affect whether Social Security is part of the picture at all. That's a detail many people don't discover until it's too late. Add in college expenses for kids, support for an aging parent, and the question of whether your current home is truly where you plan to stay long-term, and the plan quickly becomes more than a simple savings target.

Deploying the plan here means making deliberate choices while time is still on your side. It may involve increasing retirement contributions, being thoughtful about whether paying off the mortgage early actually helps, and testing the plan at the earliest possible retirement age. If the numbers work at sixty-two, they'll only improve at sixty-five. Deployment also means planning for risks that don't show up neatly on a spreadsheet—like the possibility of long-term care. Without addressing that risk, even a solid plan can unravel later.

Or let's say you're a single parent in your late forties, earning around $42,000 a year. You're balancing a mortgage, some credit card debt, and the everyday demands of raising two kids. Retirement feels far away, but your concerns are immediate. What happens to your children if something happens to you? Will you ever be able to stop working? Will you be forced to rely on your kids later in life?

In a situation like this, deployment isn't about big moves—it's about order. Paying off high-interest debt comes first because it quietly drains resources you'll need elsewhere. Emergency savings may need to be strengthened before retirement savings can grow meaningfully. Protection becomes critical. A small life insurance policy through work might feel like a start, but it's rarely enough to do what it's meant to do. Executing the plan means fixing that gap on purpose, not hoping it never matters.

Standing the watch here also includes education planning. That doesn't always mean saving large sums for college. It means understanding options, completing financial aid forms correctly, reviewing award letters carefully, and knowing when to appeal them. These steps don't require wealth. They require guidance and follow-through.

These two situations look very different because each and every one of our lives is different, but the principle is the same: Be prepared.

Course Correction: Standing the Watch

A retirement plan isn't deployed once and forgotten. It's deployed continuously, meaning pieces of the puzzle are regularly moved around when the picture changes. Markets change. Tax laws change. Health and family needs change. Standing the watch means staying engaged, checking the instruments, and making adjustments early—before small problems turn into big ones.

What might these course corrections look like?

Sometimes the trigger is market-related, even for clients whose plans were designed to limit exposure to market swings. Let's say a retired couple is drawing income from sources chosen specifically to provide stability, not growth. On paper, their exposure to day-to-day market movement is minimal. But even well-built plans can feel pressure when a major downturn hits at the wrong time. In situations like that, we may temporarily adjust where income is coming from—leaning more heavily on stable sources while giving growth-oriented assets time to recover. I've seen a small, early adjustment make a meaningful difference in both outcomes and peace of mind.

Other times, the trigger is employment. Let's say someone loses a job in their late fifties and assumes their only option is to tap a retirement account early and take the penalty. Standing the watch means knowing when that isn't necessary. In some cases, the rules allow access to certain workplace retirement funds without the usual 10 percent penalty—if you know how and when to use them. I've seen people avoid costly mistakes simply by slowing down, understanding their options, and choosing the right lever to pull.

Taxes can also force a course correction. A change in tax law or a shift in how Social Security benefits are taxed can quietly erode cash flow if no one is paying attention. Standing the watch means catching those changes early and adjusting withdrawals, contribution strategies, or timing decisions before they become painful. I've worked with families who assumed their tax picture was "set," only to realize later that a few small tweaks could have saved them thousands.

Life events often demand the biggest adjustments. Divorce, for example, can turn a stable financial picture upside down overnight. Debt may be divided unevenly. Credit may take a hit. In especially complicated situations, one spouse's bankruptcy can ripple into the other's future plans. Standing the watch here means focusing on solvency and stability first—making sure the plan still works, even if it looks different from before. I've seen people regain peace of mind not because everything was perfect but because they finally had a clear path forward again.

Health changes matter too. Maybe one spouse retires earlier than planned due to medical issues, or ongoing care becomes part of the picture. Or perhaps a family is navigating the loss of a spouse while also caring for a child with special needs. In moments like these, the plan has to go beyond numbers. Income, benefits, taxes, and long-term support all intersect with deeply personal decisions. Standing the watch means recognizing that planning is still happening even when life feels overwhelming and making sure no one has to navigate it alone.

It's also true that course corrections aren't always driven by hardship. A business may do better than expected. Someone may work longer than planned. Expenses can turn out to be lower than projected. In those moments, adjustment could mean increasing income, improving legacy plans, or simply giving someone permission to enjoy what they've worked so hard to build. I've seen people gain confidence simply by realizing they had more margin than they thought.

This is why ongoing oversight matters. Retirement planning isn't about predicting every turn ahead—it's about being ready to respond when the course shifts. When someone is standing the watch, small adjustments stay small. Left unattended, they rarely do.

That's the difference between having a plan on paper and having a plan that actually works.

Bringing It All Together

By the time you reach this stage, the goal isn't complexity—it's confidence. We've reached the part when preparation becomes real, when a plan stops being a collection of ideas and starts doing its job. The heavy lifting has already been done. What remains is execution, attention, and follow-through.

A well-built retirement plan doesn't promise that nothing will ever change. It assumes things will. Markets will move. Laws will shift. Life will throw surprises at you—good and bad. The purpose of deployment isn't to eliminate those changes. It's to make sure that you're ready for them and that when adjustments are needed, they're thoughtful instead of rushed.

And while some of what you've read in this chapter reflects how we work with our own clients, the principles themselves are universal. Whether you work with us or with another professional, this is what planning done right looks like: clear priorities, deliberate execution, and ongoing oversight.

Retirement isn't a finish line you cross once. It's a phase you live in, sometimes for decades. The plans that hold up best aren't the ones that looked perfect on day one. They're the ones that were built to adapt.

When preparation is solid, execution is thoughtful, and someone is standing the watch, you don't have to fear what's ahead. You can focus on living the life you worked so hard to build—confident that your plan is doing exactly what it was designed to do.

THIS ISN'T A SOLO VOYAGE

I'm sure you've realized by now that retirement planning isn't about finding the perfect formula. It's about learning how to see clearly, make good decisions with the information you have, and stay steady when conditions change. Over the course of your life, you've already navigated a career or two, family responsibilities, health concerns, and financial choices—often without a clear map. What we've been doing together is raising the periscope, getting our bearings, and choosing a course that makes sense for where you are now and where you want to go.

Good planning doesn't eliminate uncertainty. It gives you context. It helps you understand what matters most, what risks actually need attention, and which worries can be set aside. When the plan is built well and monitored carefully, financial decisions stop feeling like emergencies and start feeling manageable. That's when stress begins to ease and peace of mind has room to take hold.

One thing I've learned over the years is that no one should try to make this voyage alone. The idea that you're supposed to figure everything out by yourself has never made much sense to me. On a submarine, nothing important is done solo. Everyone has a role. Everyone watches their instruments. And when something changes, the crew responds together. Retirement planning works the same way.

My role has always been to serve as a steady presence helping you think through decisions, understand your options, and make adjustments when life shifts course. I don't see this work as a transaction but as a partnership. The greatest satisfaction I get from what I do isn't found in charts or statements—it's in seeing a plan make a real, positive difference in someone's life. Reducing anxiety. Restoring confidence. Helping someone sleep better at night knowing they're not drifting without a heading.

I also believe strongly that the right relationship has to feel right. If at any point you decide I'm not the best person to help you navigate your situation, I'm willing to help you find someone who is. That's not a failure—it's part of doing this job with integrity. Those conversations don't end relationships. More often than not, they turn into handshakes, friendships, and familiar faces around town.

There's a saying I've carried with me for a long time: Work until you don't have to introduce yourself. To me, that's not about recognition. It's about consistency. Showing up. Doing the work the right way, year after year, so trust is earned quietly and steadily, just like a well-run ship.

That same mindset is why I try to share what I know beyond my office. Whether I'm sitting across from a family or explaining financial concepts on local television in plain language, the goal is always the same: clarity without confusion, honesty without hype. People deserve straight answers they can understand.

If at some point you'd like to continue the conversation, we would welcome it! Reaching out doesn't commit you to anything—it's simply a chance to talk, ask questions, and see whether what we do makes sense for you. From there, we can decide together what the next step ought to be.

You can learn more about us or get in touch at **outlookfc.com**, or reach our office directly by phone at **(937) 552-9990**. If email is easier, you can always reach us at **support@outlookfc.com**.

However you choose to connect, the goals are the same: a straightforward conversation, clear answers, and a sense of whether this feels like the right next move for you.

No matter where you are on your journey—just starting out, nearing retirement, or already living in it—you don't have to navigate it alone. The waters will change.

The weather will shift. That's life. But with a clear heading, a solid plan, and someone standing the watch with you, there's no reason to fear what lies ahead.

This isn't a solo voyage, and it never was.

ABOUT THE AUTHOR

 ROB BURNETTE leads Outlook Financial Center in case design, investment management, and daily operations. He has worked in financial services since 1985 and is licensed to offer investment advice and insurance products.

As a registered tax preparer with the IRS, Rob participates in the Annual Filing Season Program and is certified as a National Social Security Advisor. He graduated from the US Naval Academy with a Bachelor of Science in Electrical Engineering, earned an MBA from the University of New Haven, and holds a Financial Planning certificate from Kaplan University.

Rob's professional memberships include the International Association of Registered Financial Consultants, Million Dollar Round Table—Top of the Table, and Ed Slott's Master Elite IRA Advisor Group. He has contributed to many publications, including *USA Today*, *Barron's*, *Forbes*, MarketWatch, WDTN Dayton, and WHIO Dayton. He is a 2017 alumnus of Leadership Troy Ohio and is passionate about supporting kids' sports programs, 4-H, and FFA.

This is his first book.